Favourite Themes

Jenni Tavener

Bright Ideas
FOR Early Years

Published by Scholastic Publications Ltd,
Villiers House, Clarendon Avenue,
Leamington Spa, Warwickshire
CV32 5PR

© 1995 Scholastic Publications
Text © 1995 Jenni Tavener

Author Jenni Tavener
Editor Noel Pritchard
Assistant editor Kate Banham
Designer Tracey Ramsey
Illustrator Jon Higham
Photographs by Martin Sookias
Grateful thanks to the staff and pupils of
Saint Christopher's Primary School, Coventry,
who are featured in these photographs.

Cover design by Sue Stockbridge
Cover photograph by Fiona Pragoff

Typeset by Typesetters (Birmingham) Ltd
Artwork by David Harban Design, Warwick
Printed at Alden Press Ltd, Oxford and Northampton,
Great Britain

British Library Cataloguing in Publication Data
A catalogue record for this book is available from the British
Library

ISBN 0-590-53307-X

For Hedley

Contents

Introduction

This book is divided into eight chapters on the popular themes of: 'Growth', 'Myself', 'Pets', 'Colours', 'Shapes', 'Toys', 'Wheels' and 'Nursery Rhymes'.

Each chapter highlights activities which link directly with the topic heading and cover a wide range of curriculum areas, including the 'hidden curriculum' – caring, sharing and teamwork. Each activity is further supported by follow-up ideas. The topics can be used as a framework of activities for teachers who wish to use an integrated approach or for stimulating ideas when planning a class project. Alternatively, the topics can be 'dipped into' rather like a recipe book and used as a resource for independent activities as each one is complete in itself.

One of the main aims of the book is to offer a range of concepts that can be adapted or extended to suit the particular needs of the children.

Why use a topic-based approach?

A topic-based approach to teaching can help to promote a feeling of unity amongst a group of children as they are all working together on a shared theme. One of the enjoyable aspects of project work is that it gives children a real purpose for collecting and using information for themselves and their peers. Children's interest in a theme will develop even further when they are encouraged to draw upon their own views and experiences, as this helps them to feel totally involved and comfortable in the knowledge that their personal contributions will be of value.

We all aim to provide situations in which every child will achieve and succeed. It is useful, therefore, during the planning and evaluation stages to consider how we can best fulfil this aim and how a topic-based approach can be used to help individuals feel successful.

Below we list five underlying aims of topic work (not in order of priority), but many others will be special to each school, nursery or situation.

A topic-based approach can be used to:
- encourage creative expression;
- provide opportunities for using problem-solving skills;
- encourage children to experiment and evaluate;
- develop children's awareness of their environment;
- encourage a sense of team effort and co-operation.

Integration

An integrated approach to class work enables a natural flow to occur between subject areas. A three-dimensional robot made during a craft session, for example, can provide a first-hand source for measuring and a realistic reason for comparing results (to find out whose robot is the tallest, shortest, widest and so on). The unique appearance of each model can help to encourage descriptive language and provide a rich and original resource for imaginative stories, plays and poems.

The interest developed during one task can stimulate an enthusiasm for further relevant activities and an effective progression of work can then develop from the children's enjoyment in learning.

Displaying topic work

The presentation of children's topic work within their school or nursery is very important. An imaginative environment, which is rich in display and full of the children's own work, can help to enhance each child's sense of belonging and involvement. Creating such an environment helps the children to feel proud of their achievements and illustrates to the 'audience' (parents, staff, visitors and other children) that the pupils' efforts are valued.

Displays can therefore play a valuable role in improving the children's learning environment and in promoting an enthusiasm for a topic or theme. Throughout this book ideas for interesting and creative displays are given, all based on the children's own work.

Myself

Chapter one

A topic on 'Myself' can include a vast range of activities to help children become more aware of themselves, their peers and others around them.

The first group of activities in this chapter focus on the child as an individual then move on to some of the physical attributes of the human body. These will provide the children with the opportunity to develop their investigation skills and gain a greater awareness of how their bodies work.

The emotional side of children's natures is then broached, via activities such as 'Feelings' and 'Happy/sad mask'. These can be used to help reinforce co-operation and understanding the needs of others. Themes relating to health and hygiene can extend from the structured play ideas at the end of this chapter.

Birthday chart

Objectives
To assist the children in remembering their birth date and the months of the year. To reinforce counting skills.

What you need
Pens, paper or card, collage equipment, crayons, paints.

What to do
Invite the children to draw a shape (approximately 30cm square in size) on to paper or card, to represent a birthday parcel. Let them cut this shape out and then decorate it by designing their own wrapping using crayons, paints or collage. Can they write their own name tag to place on the parcel?

Write the months of the year along the edge of a large sheet of paper. The children can then place their parcel next to their own birthday month. Display the resulting chart on the wall and use as a resource for counting.

Follow-up
● Each child can make, wrap and label a small three-dimensional 'parcel'. Place these in one of 12 open-sided boxes previously marked with the names of the months. Use this as an interactive display for practical sorting and counting activities. For example, asking the children to place their small parcel in their 'birthday month' box. How many are in each month?
● Provide a selection of coloured card for the children to design original birthday cards and badges.
● Play some of the children's favourite birthday party games.
● Make a wall frieze based on 'the birthday tea table'. Pin a real tablecloth on the wall as a background for the children's paintings of party food. To give a three-dimensional effect, mount their pictures on to small boxes and include real balloons, crackers and streamers. Help the children write their own place name cards to add to the display.
● Hold a dolls' birthday party.
● Involve the children in making party hats. Let them design their own style. Then hold a party hat parade.

Baby booklets

Objective
To develop self-awareness.

What you need
Card, baby photographs, adhesive, pens, pencils.

What to do
Ask the children to bring in a photograph of themselves as a baby. Help them each to make a little photo-booklet by folding a piece of card in half and sticking their picture inside. Personal details can be added such as name, birthday, weight when born and so on. Use this booklet to stimulate discussion about similarities and differences between the children as babies and as they are now, for example their size, the physical things they can do which a baby cannot, the food they eat, clothing, sleep and speech.

Follow-up

● Ask someone to bring their baby into the class or nursery. The children will enjoy watching it play, feed or having a bath.

● Help the children make a 'Me now' booklet with a recent photograph of themselves on the front cover. Invite them to include drawings or writing about the things they are proud of being able to do, such as getting dressed, using a knife and fork, running fast.

● Set up an imaginative play area as a 'baby clinic'.

● Let the children construct a mobile, toy or rattle for a baby.

● Talk about baby animals. Introduce the correct names used to describe young animals.

● Bring a baby animal into the class or visit a farm, pet shop or zoo.

● Discuss with the children why young animals and children need special care and why they are dependent on others.

● Make a class book entitled 'Babies need help with . . .'.

Height chart

Objective
To encourage children to make comparisons in height.

What you need
Long strips of paper, scissors, sticky labels, crayons.

What to do
Let the children help each other to make a strip of paper the same length as their height. Secure these lengths with a name label to the wall to show the children's heights. Comparing heights can be rather difficult for young children as the top of

their head is 'out of sight'. To make it more fun, ask each child to draw a picture of their nose on a sticky label then help them attach this in the correct position on their strip of paper. They will enjoy finding out where their nose is in relation to their peers'!

Follow-up

● Use the chart to set practical challenges, for example 'How many noses are higher than yours?', 'Find a nose the same height as yours'.

● Encourage the children to collect data on hair and eye colour and help them make a class bar chart.

● Let the children work together to compare the height of their knees, shoulders and waist. Help them to add these measurements to their height chart with labels stating: 'My knees came up to here', 'My waist comes up to here' and so on.

● Challenge the children to find out if the tallest child is the longest child when lying down.

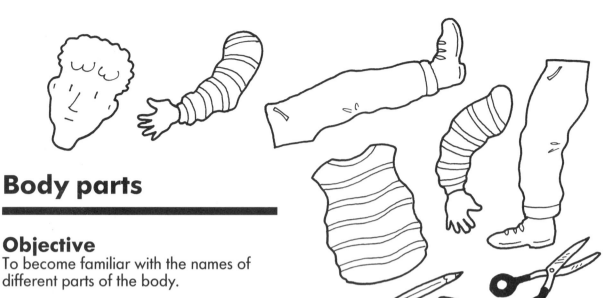

Body parts

Objective
To become familiar with the names of different parts of the body.

What you need
Card, pens, scissors.

What to do
Help the children to make a life-size 'body part' jigsaw by drawing round and cutting out the shape of one child on thin card. Divide the outline into various body parts for the children to re-assemble. The number of parts will depend on the age and ability of the class. Encourage the children to name the different parts of the body as they piece the jigsaw together. Ask them to look at their own body. Discuss which parts move and bend. Help them identify their joints — knees, wrists, knuckles and so on. Talk about the names and uses of joints.

Follow-up
● Play the 'Body parts matching game' (for two players or two teams).

What you need
Two life-size jigsaws (one for each player or team). A selection of picture cards — each card should illustrate a part of the body; the number of cards should match the number of parts of the jigsaw. These can be drawn by the children or cut from photos or magazine pictures.

What to do
Assemble both jigsaws. Place all the picture cards face down in a pile. The two players/teams should take turns to remove a picture card from the top of the pile. If the first player reveals say, a hand, he/she is allowed to remove one hand from their jigsaw, the card is then returned to the bottom of the pile. The process is repeated by the second player/team. The winner is the first to remove all their jigsaw pieces.

A box of measurements

Objective
To develop skills and interest in matching, comparing and measuring by producing a practical and personal record of measurements.

What you need
Card, wide ribbon, sticky tape, scissors, a selection of boxes, bags or large envelopes.

What to do

Ask the children to make cut-out shapes of their hands and feet from card. Help each child to cut two lengths of ribbon. One should match the length of their arm, the other the length of their leg. Now ask the children to secure their cut-out hand and foot to the appropriate lengths of ribbon. Help them to measure their lengths of ribbon in metric or arbitrary units.

A box, bag or envelope will enable the children to take their 'ribbon measurements' home, or to store them for the follow-up activities.

Follow-up

● Ask the children to compare arm and leg lengths with their friends.
● Set challenges such as 'Find out if the child with the longest arm is also the tallest child.'
● Draw round one child, mount the cut-out shape on the wall at the child's own height. Hang three or four ribbons of varying lengths next to the display (one of which is the correct length for the arm or leg). Challenge the children to use their matching skills to identify the correct lengths of ribbon.
● Introduce a metre stick. Challenge the children to find items in the room which are taller, shorter, narrower, wider than one metre.
● Use the metre length in PE. Ask the children to find out how many of their steps fit along one metre? What about giant steps, jumps, tiptoes, hops and so on?

Fingerprint people

Objectives

To encourage close attention to detail. To show that every fingerprint is unique.

What you need

A strip of paper for each child approximately 10cm x 50cm folded into a five page zig-zag book, a washable ink pad, felt-tipped pens, a magnifying glass.

What to do

Encourage the children to use the magnifying glass to look at details on their fingers. Extend this by looking at the similarities and differences between each other's prints.

Supervise each child as they make a print of each finger of one hand on each page of their zig-zag book (one print per page). Using the felt-tipped pens, let them create characters for the prints, such as Mr Thumb, Maggie Middle Finger, Baby Little Finger. The children will enjoy making up stories about their characters. Make sure that the children wash their hands thoroughly after this activity.

Follow-up

● Use the magnifying glass to study other body details such as hair, fingernails and eyes.
● Co-ordinate this activity with an educational visit from your local police liaison officer, to talk about how they use fingerprints to help catch criminals.

Feely bag

Objective
To increase awareness about the sense of touch and to develop skills in investigation and description.

What you need
A collection of familiar objects (ensure the items are varied in shape, size, weight and texture), a drawstring bag or box with a covered arm hole.

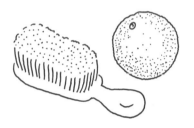 

What to do
Display the collection of objects for the children to see and feel. After they have had a chance to do this remove the objects from sight and hide one item in the feely bag. Invite the children to feel inside the bag to discover which object has been hidden. Extend this further by asking the children to describe what they are feeling. Can their friends guess the object from the description given?

Follow-up
• Make two identical collections of fabric (velvet, corduroy, silk, cotton, netting, fur). Ensure that all the swatches are the same size and shape. Stick one collection on a strip of card and display this for the children to see and feel. Place one swatch from the second collection inside the feely bag. Now challenge the children to find out which piece of material is hidden in the bag. Swatches of paper could be used instead (card, tissue, embossed wallpaper, foil).

• Involve the children in making a 'feely' picture. For example, a large mouse with felt or fur fabric for the body, silky material for the ears, buttons for the eyes and nose, straws for the whiskers. Use the picture to play a game similar to 'pin the tail on the donkey', only this time they can pin the whiskers on the mouse. The different textures will provide 'feely' clues when the children are blindfolded.

• Talk about Braille for the blind. Discuss the other senses a blind person might rely on, such as the sense of sound.

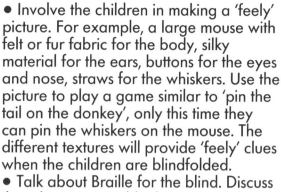 

• Make a tape-recording of familiar sounds for the children to identify (a doorbell, footsteps, a car hooting).

• Encourage the children to record their own set of familiar sounds in the school or nursery (the whistle or bell, singing, putting chairs up, washing paint brushes).

• Set up a sound table with a variety of objects which make a noise. In pairs, invite the children to play sound identification games.

Portrait floor cushion

Objective
To provide a sense of belonging and to create something useful.

What you need
Two pieces of plain fabric approximately one metre square, a selection of permanent colour markers, masking tape, newspaper, needles and thread, pens, paper, a small mirror, cushion stuffing.

What to do

Lay one of the sheets of fabric on to a table and secure the edges with masking tape. (Newspaper under the fabric will help to protect the table.) Let the children take turns to sign their name and draw their portrait on to the fabric using a permanent marker. Invite them to practise on a piece of paper first. A small mirror will encourage close observation. When complete, the children can help to sew the two pieces of fabric together and stuff this to make a personalised floor cushion for the book corner.

Follow-up

● Using fabric paint, let the children make hand and foot print patterns on to fabric. Help them to turn their printed material into curtains and cushions for the classroom or 'home corner'.
● The children can contribute writing and/or drawings to a class sequence book or poster describing how they made the cushion and curtains.
● Look at portraits and profiles on stamps, cameos, coins and old masters paintings.
● Use an overhead projector to produce shadow profiles of the children. Draw round and cut out these profiles. Mount these on contrasting coloured paper.

Happy/sad mask

Objective

To help develop self-expression.

What you need

Circles of card approximately 20cm in diameter with a crescent moon shape removed from the centre, pencils, crayons, mirrors.

What to do

Talk with the children about their most happy memories. Why were they happy? Who or what made them happy? Ask the children to think of a time when they helped to make someone feel happy. Who was it? What did they do?

Now invite the children to look at themselves in a mirror. Ask them to make a happy face. Encourage them to describe what happens to their mouth, eyes and cheeks. Present each child with one of the card shapes to examine. Challenge them to find a 'happy face' and a 'sad face' on the card. Let them twist and turn the card to find the two 'faces'. They can then use crayons to create a two-sided mask to use in the follow-up activities.

Follow-up

● Make a recording of lively dance music occasionally interrupted with slow sombre music. The children will enjoy moving and dancing to the music while swapping their mask around to match the mood created.
● Let the children wear their mask while miming the actions of a sad or happy character. For example: how would a happy/sad person walk, sit, wave and so on?
● Talk about other expressions, such as anger, surprise and boredom.

Feelings

Objective
To encourage the children to develop empathy.

What you need
Photocopiable page 88, 'What are they feeling?'

What to do
Let the children ponder over the pictures on the photocopiable sheet. Ask them to look closely. What do they think the children are feeling and why? Give them time to explain their views in their own words. Invite them to share their own experiences of feeling lost, hurt, lonely, bored, excited, surprised and happy.

Children who are able to write can make simple speech bubbles to go with the pictures on the photocopiable page.

Follow-up
● Talk about caring for others less fortunate than ourselves.
● Let the children contribute writing or drawings to a class book entitled 'I helped . . .'. For example 'I helped mummy wash up', 'I helped my friend when she fell over'.
● Talk about 'people who help us' in the community (ambulance people, firefighters, police and so on).
● Invite the lollipop person or other familiar helper to talk to the children about what they do.

In disguise

Objective
To help develop self-confidence through role-play.

What you need
Dressing-up clothes, a long mirror, face crayons, pens, scissors, paper, till, money (real or pretend), space for a 'stage', chairs.

What to do
Set up a class 'theatre' with a 'stage' and seating area for an 'audience'. Help the children to number the seats and make 'theatre seat tickets'. These tickets can be 'sold' at a 'box office'. Invite the children to experiment with the dressing-up clothes and spend some time in disguise. Some children may wish to emulate a story character, others may choose to be someone famous. Help them to act out short scenes from their favourite book, or rehearse a song, joke or poem.

Some young children are very self-conscious, however being in disguise often helps to inspire those who are particularly shy about acting in front of others.

Follow-up

● Take photographs of the children all wearing the same disguise, such as a pirate's scarf, an eye patch and moustache. Mount the pictures in a book or on the wall. The children will have fun trying to identify their own photo amongst all the others.
● Encourage the children to explain how they recognise themselves. What personal features give clues as to their real identity – hair colour, eye colour?
● Play the 'Changing appearance number game'.

What you need
For three players: three hats, three wigs, three pairs of glasses, each labelled 1–3; a die with dots 1–3 and three blank faces.

What to do
The first player throws the die. If, say, a 3 is shown, he collects and wears the hat, wig or pair of glasses labelled '3' and passes the die to the next player. If a blank side is shown he misses that turn. The players take it in turn to throw the die. The winner is the first child to collect one wig, one hat and one pair of glasses.

This game is very versatile. Any combination of clothing can be used. Hilarious results can emerge if you mix and match three outfits, for example a clown, a policeman and a ballet dancer. Relate the number values to the age and ability of the children. To reinforce addition or subtraction, use two dice.

Favourite plate of food

Objective
To increase food awareness and manipulative skills.

What you need
Modelling dough (two cups of flour to one cup of salt plus water), paint, varnish, a selection of real foods, pictures of food, paper plates.

What to do
Prepare an area in your classroom or nursery to stimulate discussion by displaying colourful pictures and posters of food. Capture the children's interest by including a selection of real foods. Provoke their inquisitive nature by including something unusual such as an exotic fruit, perhaps a gourd, or a mis-shapen carrot. Invite the children to discuss their favourite food. Does everyone have the same likes and dislikes?

Using the soft dough, let the children freely shape, mould and model representations of their favourite foods. When dry, let them paint their 'food' by mixing their own colours. Help them to varnish their finished work and display this on paper plates.

Follow up

• Use the model food in a class shop for buying and selling activities.
• Introduce the theme of healthy eating and a balanced diet. Talk about food safety, allergies and food eaten by different religions or cultural groups.
• Set up a tasting panel. Can the children identify different flavours (sweet, sour, salty, bitter). Be aware of food allergies.
• Change the colour of flavoured jelly using food colouring – does the colour change affect the perception of flavour?

The doctor's surgery

Objectives

To help children to work and play effectively in co-operation with others. To help develop social awareness.

What you need

A small child's bed or couch, blankets, a table, chair, telephone, paper, pencils, a nurse's outfit or hat, a white shirt for a 'doctor', a stethoscope (preferably real), empty syringes, bandages, scissors, cotton wool, pretend medicine (coloured water), plastic spoons.

What to do

Stimulate imaginative play by involving the children in the setting-up of a 'surgery' or 'hospital' in the home corner. They can help decide where the equipment should be placed, where the doctor should sit and arrange the seating in the 'waiting room'. Include provision for emergent writing by providing pens and paper for the children to write 'prescriptions', 'notes', 'patients' names' and 'appointments'.

Follow-up

• Talk with the children about keeping well, exercise and hygiene (for instance, washing hands before a meal, brushing teeth).
• Paint some posters on the theme of hygiene.
• Make 'get well' cards for children who are off sick.
• Let the children listen to their own heartbeat using a real stethoscope.
• Invite the school nurse in to talk to the children about her job.
• Alternative ideas for imaginative play areas relevant to a topic on 'Myself' could include a 'baby clinic', an 'optician's', a 'dolls' hospital', a 'medical room', a 'dentist's', a 'chemist's' or a 'shoe shop'.

Toys

Chapter two

A topic on 'Toys' can be very exciting for young children. Every child is curious about toys as they are often very much in touch with the latest commercial products and are fascinated to find out about making their own.

The activities in this chapter aim to capture this fascination by providing the children with a wide variety of opportunities to construct and create their own toys. Such work provides an invaluable resource for stimulating the children's interest and inspiring their imagination, and can be used as a springboard to introduce and extend skills in all areas of the curriculum.

Sorting real toys

Objective
To reinforce sorting, matching and set-making skills and to develop mathematical language.

What you need
An assortment of real toys.

What to do
Encourage the children to bring in some of their own toys. Discuss the different attributes of the toys and help the children to think about how the toys can be grouped. Involve the children in practical set-making by either asking them to make their own set, such as 'Make a set of toys which have wheels' or by giving them a set to identify. Explain that more than one phrase may describe the set correctly.

Follow-up
● Use the toys for close observational drawing or painting.
● Read some stories which involve toys or teddies, such as Jane Hissey's bear books or 'Goldilocks and the Three Bears'.
● Involve the children in making a set of 12 picture cards (three bears, three chairs, three bowls, three beds) which they can use to play a matching game based on the story of 'Goldilocks and the Three Bears'.

What to do
Three players opt to collect either Daddy Bear and his belongings, Mummy Bear and her belongings or Baby Bear and his belongings. Lay all the cards out face down in front of the players, who then take turns to turn one over. The players may keep cards that form part of their set and replace cards that do not match. The first player to collect a complete set of four cards is the winner.

Teddy biscuits

Objective
To provide the experience of preparing and cooking food and to stimulate discussion.

What you need
Ingredients: 125g butter, 125g sugar, 250g plain flour, 1 beaten egg, currants and cherry pieces. *Utensils:* an oven, teddy-shaped pastry cutters, baking trays, a rolling pin, fork, weighing scales, bowl, spoon, sieve, aprons.

What to do
Make sure the children wash their hands before they begin. Then follow these instructions:
1. Sieve the flour into a bowl.
2. Rub in the butter.
3. Mix in the sugar.
4. Mix in the beaten egg to form a dough.
5. Roll out the dough and cut into teddy shapes with the pastry cutters.
6. Add two currants for eyes.
7. Add a cherry for the nose.
8. Place on a greased baking tray.
9. Cook at 180°C/350°F/gas mark 4 for approximately 15 minutes.

Let the children help to weigh, sieve and mix the ingredients. Assist them while they roll and cut the mixture.

Stimulate discussion during the preparation stages by asking the children to describe what is happening to the consistency of the mixture. Talk about why it needs to be rolled and why the tray needs greasing. Highlight aspects such as safety and hygiene.

Follow-up
● Discuss the sequence of events during the preparation stages and let the children record this sequence in writing or pictures on a single sheet of paper or card. Cover the work in sticky-backed plastic or place in a clear folder and use as the first page of a classroom cook book.
● Set up a toys' tea party or teddies' picnic. Involve the children in making the sandwiches. Invite them to bring their toys or teddies to school to join in with the picnic.
● Inspire the children to write or draw party invitations to give to their parents and friends.
● Let the children make pictorial menus of the foods for the picnic. Some children will also enjoy inventing unusual names for the foods on their menus.

Jointed teddies

Objective
To develop skills in technology and help motivate creative thinking.

What you need
Card, pens, crayons, felt-tipped pens or pencils, paper-fasteners, scissors, fur fabric, adhesive.

What to do
Encourage the children to draw a large teddy to fill an A3 sheet of card. Let them draw teddy's face, colour in the shape and then cut it out. Some children may need assistance to cut card. The back of the teddy can then be coloured and fur fabric added to the ears and chest. Help the children to cut off the arms and legs and re-attach them with paper-fasteners to simulate the joints between the limbs. Older or more able children may enjoy including knee and elbow joints.

Follow-up
● Involve the children in making an A3 'pocket per page' book, about teddy (see Figures 1 and 2). The teddy's limbs can be moved to reflect the wording, for example 'Teddy is running', 'Teddy is waving'.
● Add a strip of card to the back of the teddy and loosen the joints to allow freedom of movement for dancing or for use as a shadow puppet (see Figure 3).

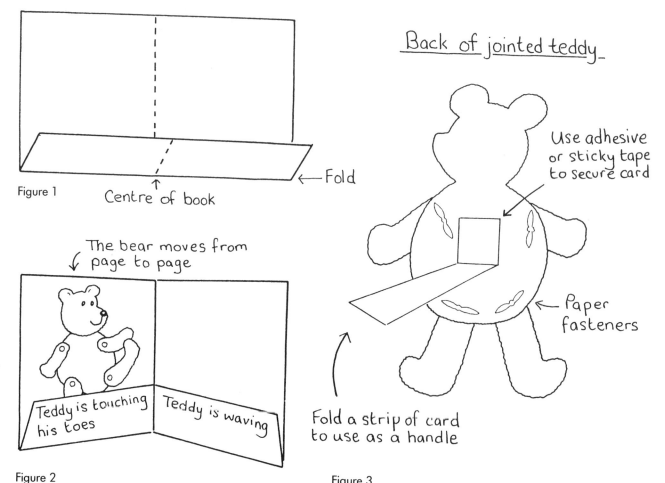

Figure 1

Centre of book

← Fold

The bear moves from page to page

Teddy is touching his toes

Teddy is waving

Figure 2

Back of jointed teddy

Use adhesive or sticky tape to secure card

← Paper fasteners

Fold a strip of card to use as a handle

Figure 3

Three-dimensional robots

Objective
To inspire imagination and extend three-dimensional model making skills.

What you need
A selection of boxes (cut open then turned inside out and stuck back together to make painting and sticking easier), adhesive, scissors, paints, a wide selection of craft materials (card, coloured sticky paper, foil paper, lolly sticks, cotton reels, sticky tape, buttons, pipe-cleaners), Lego (or other construction material), real toys.

What to do
Introduce the activity by looking at some commercial robots, transformer toys or the children's own Lego models. These toys and models can be used to inspire the children's own ideas for constructing a class 'giant robot' using the materials above. They will enjoy using their imagination to create an 'instrument panel' with lights, buttons, dials, flaps and levers.

Use the class robot to inspire the children to make their own smaller models.

Follow-up
• Help the children to measure the robots and then to display them in order of height or width.
• Talk about the names of the two-dimensional and three-dimensional shapes used on the models.
• Inspire the children to invent original stories about the robots. Provide a story 'beginning' as this will help stimulate the children's own ideas for a 'middle' and an 'ending'. The following example can be used or adapted: 'When it was dark and the moon was shining, I heard a terrible noise. I looked out of my bedroom window and saw two red lights gleaming. It was . . .'.

Robotic music

Objective
To encourage an awareness of how different sounds and instruments can be made.

What you need
Toy robots, percussion instruments, straws, corrugated card, pots, strong sticky tape, beads, lentils, rice, buttons, wool, plastic bottles, fabric, paper, ice-cream and margarine containers, dowelling, elastic bands, small boxes.

What to do
Listen to the noises made by toy robots and discuss with the children the sounds they think their own model robot would make. Share words which describe these sounds. Invite the children to create 'new' sounds using percussion instruments.

Encourage the children to make their own instruments. Suggestions may include:
— Make pan pipes by inserting straws of varying lengths into a small strip of corrugated card.
— Make maracas by taping two yoghurt pots together. The children can experiment with the sounds they can make by putting different objects inside the pots.
— Make various types of shakers by threading beads, buttons and other objects on to wool or string.
— Make scrapers by rubbing an assortment of objects along the ridges of a plastic bottle. Let the children investigate how the sounds change depending on the objects used.
— Make drums by stretching plastic, fabric, paper or other material across the top of any hollow container. The children may need adult help to secure the edges with strong tape. They can also make an assortment of 'drumsticks' for soft or loud sounds by taping or tying soft or hard objects to the ends of dowelling.
— Make instruments to 'pluck' by stretching elastic bands around an empty plastic box. Different thicknesses of band or the depth of box used will alter the sound when plucked.

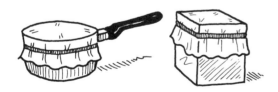

Follow-up
● Let the children experiment together with their instruments to help each other 'compose' original robot music.
● Help the children to record their robot sounds, both verbal and instrumental.
● Use the instruments or the recordings during drama sessions to inspire robotic actions and movements.

Robotic movements

Objectives
To stimulate an interest in expressive mime or dance. To listen and respond to instructions.

What you need
A room with space for the children to move around freely and safely.

What to do
Create a story about a toy robot which comes to life. Incorporate many opportunities for the children to act out the part of the robot, improvising robotic movements. The following offers an outline which can be adapted and extended with the children's own ideas.

It is the story of a toy robot, who is stored in the corner of a toy shop. He has to sit very still all day and gets very lonely and bored. He looks forward to night time when the shop is closed and empty, because when it is dark and no one can see him, he can have fun whizzing around the shop floor. He has to start slowly.

Invite the children to stand very still, pretending that they are the robot in the corner of the shop. Then continue.

First, the robot presses his nose. Encourage the children to press their own nose and explain that this controls the robot's face. Now he can open and shut his eyes, twitch his nose, open and close his mouth and so on. Next he tweaks his ears — this enables him to move his head up and down, and left to right. Next he pushes his chin — this enables him to bend at the waist and twist from side to side (feet remain still). Finally, a touch of the tummy button makes the robot walk slowly in stiff, jerky movements. A pretend control panel on their chest can be used to make them move faster, slower, jump, stop, gnash teeth, spin arms and so on.

Encourage the children to think of some jobs for the robot to do. For example, pack shelves, sweep the floor and move toys.

Bring the activity to a close by explaining that when it begins to get light, the robot has to return to his corner and turn himself 'off' so that when the shop opens, no one knows that he can move. The children can then turn themselves 'off' by reversing the instructions – push their tummy button to stop walking, push their chin to stand up straight, tweak their ear to centre their head, push their nose to keep their face still.

Follow-up
● To reinforce listening skills and help the children gain confidence in giving instructions, encourage simple role-play situations where one child mimes the part of a robot, while their partner gives the 'commands'.
● Turn your home corner into a 'space station' with a large tabletop control panel. The children will enjoy making this by sticking raised objects on to some sheets of card and covering this in silver foil or silver paint. Make 'windows' using picture posters of the Earth as seen from space. Outside, hang child-made 'stars' and 'moons'.
● Make robot costumes using large boxes and tubes.
● Let the children take turns to dress up as a robot during role-play or for imaginative play while in their class 'space station'.

Back view: Fold a strip of card to use as a handle

Figure 1

Hand puppets

Objective
To stimulate language development and creative thinking through puppet play.

What you need
Card, crayons, felt-tipped pens, pencils, scissors, sticky tape.

What to do
Stimulate the children's interest by reading a favourite monster story, such as *Not Now, Bernard* by David McKee (Oliver & Boyd). They can then make their own monster puppet by drawing around their hand on to card. The monster's face with its 'glaring eyes', 'frightful nose' and 'fearsome fangs' can be added to the palm area, while the fingers can be used as 'spiky hair'. Once coloured and cut out, fix a strip of card to the back, to hold on to during creative play (see Figure 1).

Follow-up

• Make 'baby monster' finger puppets using the fingers cut from old gloves.
• Encourage the children to devise strange names for their monster puppets. Use the opportunity to reinforce descriptive language or introduce rhyming words.
• Help the children to make three-dimensional monster faces from papier mâché, clay or play dough.
• Compile a large story-book, written and illustrated with the children's own ideas about their puppets and models.
• Help the children to sew fabric hand puppets using non-fraying material. They can begin by drawing an outline of their own hand on to squared paper to produce a pattern of the right size. The paper pattern can also be used to introduce the theme of area, by counting the number of squares within the shape of each hand.

Pop-up puppets

Objective

To provide children with the opportunity of creating their own action toy and to increase their awareness of the design and technology involved.

What you need

Plastic pots with a hole in the base (such as small flower pots), dowelling, card circles slightly smaller in diameter than the plastic pot, strong tape (such as insulating tape), felt-tipped pens, fabric pieces, scissors, wool, commercial examples of a Jack-in-the-box and a pop-up puppet.

What to do

Begin by looking at some examples of a Jack-in-the-box and pop-up puppets with the children. Show them the basic

Figure 1

principle of a pop-up puppet (a card circle secured to dowelling, placed in a pot – see Figure 1). Explain that the card circle represents the 'pop-up' face. Would it be happy, surprised, funny? When the children have drawn a face, help them to tape it to the dowelling. Let them fit the dowelling in the hole in their pot and slide it freely up and down. Encourage a high degree of independence as the children use their imagination to decorate their toy.

Follow-up

• Make a collection of words to describe the actions of the pop-up puppet and Jack-in-the-box, for example spring, bounce, bob, jump.
• Use the collection of words to help the children to create simple poems, such as Spring Jack spring, Bounce Jack bounce.
• Encourage the children to make a comic strip story about their toy by dividing an A4 sheet into four or six parts. The children can then illustrate a sequence of events.
• Tape record the children's spontaneous stories as they play with their puppets.
• Listen to the spontaneous stories and invite the children to compile a picture book to complement the tape recordings.

A puppet theatre

Objective
To gain skills and confidence in working as part of a team to produce a shared classroom resource.

What you need
The theatre: a sturdy cardboard box, dowelling, pegs (standard or dolly), material, cord. *Scenery backdrops:* paper, paint, scissors, a story-book. *Story characters:* card, felt-tipped pens, scissors, adhesive, dowelling.

What to do
Note: For safety reasons all cutting of cardboard boxes should be done by an adult. The rest of the construction, however, is easy enough for young children to complete under supervision.

Making the puppet theatre:
• Let the children help open the base and the lid of the box (Figure 1).
• Punch a hole on each side of the box near to the front and insert dowelling across the top of the box (Figure 2).
• Make simple curtains by draping two lengths of material over the dowelling. Tie these back with cord or ribbon (Figure 3).
• Hang backdrops (painted by the children) quickly and easily by clipping three or four pegs to the back of the box. Cut three or four holes in the top of the backdrops to place the pegs through (Figure 4).
• Cut one slit, in either side of the box, which can be used to insert story characters (Figure 5).

The children can paint their own backdrops to illustrate scenes from stories they have made up, or chosen from the book corner. Then let them draw their own story characters to cut out and stick on to a strip of card or dowelling.

Use the 'mini theatre' with the backdrops removed for hand and finger puppet shows.

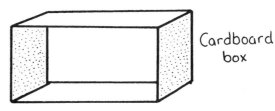
Cardboard box

Figure 1

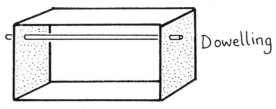
Dowelling

Figure 2

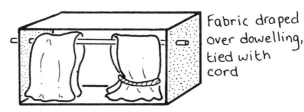
Fabric draped over dowelling, tied with cord

Figure 3

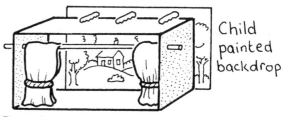
Child painted backdrop

Figure 4

Slit in side of box for story character

Figure 5

Creating a toy shop

Objective
To stimulate structured play and initiate a greater understanding of using money.

What you need
A selection of toys (some commercial, others made from construction kits and those created by the children during craft and technology sessions); tables, chairs, a till, pretend money, pens and paper, wrapping paper, bags, boxes.

What to do
Invite the children to display the toys to create a class 'toy shop'. Help them to write price tags and information labels ('for sale', 'sold', 'open', 'closed' and so on) to stand alongside the toys. The children will also enjoy decorating gift boxes and making paper bags for their toy shop.

Discuss the different events which could take place in a toy shop, such as 'buying a present', 'spending pocket money' or 'returning faulty goods'. Set up 'buying' and 'selling' situations. (The amount of money exchanged will depend on the age and ability of the children.) Use the activity to reinforce counting skills, giving change and coin recognition.

Keep a record of the children's ideas to use as a stimulus for future structured play activities.

Follow-up
● A simple money sorting tray, with separate compartments for different coins can be made by the children using shallow pots or large coffee lids placed in an open-sided cereal box. Use the tray to help matching and ordering skills.
● Discuss the meaning of words such as: 'price', 'pay', 'change', 'expensive', 'cheap', 'sale' and so on.

The lost toy

Objectives
To enhance skills in talking and listening to other people's experiences and views. To increase awareness of the children's nursery or school environment.

What you need
A comfortable place to sit.

What to do
Initiate discussion about losing a favourite toy. Have the children ever lost a toy and if so, how was it lost, did they find it and where did they find it? Do the children have a favourite toy? How would they feel if it was lost? Invite them to share their experiences and thoughts. Participate in the discussion yourself by contributing an experience of your own.

Generate further discussion about what the children would do if they found a lost item in school including where they would take it and who they would give it to.
Note: Be aware of invoking feelings of other losses, such as grief.

Follow-up
● Talk about where the school keeps 'lost property'.
● Ask the children to find out what happens to unclaimed 'lost property'.
● Involve the children in making a 'lost property' box for the classroom.

A toy town floor map

Objective
To introduce the children to simple map-making and to encourage awareness of routes and directions.

What you need
A card base, approximately one metre square, straight and curved strips of card cut by the children in a selection of colours, lengths and widths to represent roads, paths and rivers; yellow and blue powder paint and suitable tools for colour-mixing, adhesive, shoe boxes, felt-tipped pens, aprons.

What to do
Invite the children to make a 'toy town' for their dolls and toy cars. Discuss what they want to include in their 'town' and if possible take them for a walk in the local area to inspire ideas.

Let the children begin mapping out their own pattern of roads and so on by sticking the strips of card to the card base. Provide powder paint so they can mix their own shades of green for painting parks, fields and gardens. The children can construct model houses, garages, churches and so on from small boxes, to be added to the floor map.

The toy town, or map alone, can be used to stimulate imaginative play and also used to develop a sense of direction. Ask the children to work out routes for cars and pedestrians.

Follow-up
• Take the children on a walk to observe road signs and crossings.
• Talk with the children about safe places to cross the road.
• To increase awareness of road safety help the children to include zebra crossings, traffic lights or road signs on their floor map. Signs can be made easily by cutting pictures from a Highway Code booklet or by drawing the appropriate pictures on to circles and triangles of card. Use dowelling or lolly sticks to stand these upright in Plasticine.

Toys from the past

Objective
To promote an interest in and understanding of times past.

What you need
Examples of toys or games from the past; a grandparent or other older person known to the children.

What to do
Invite the children's parents and grandparents to bring in a toy they have kept from their childhood days. It might be possible to arrange a session during which a willing grandparent could talk to the children about the toys and games of years ago.

Discuss with the children how things change as time goes by. Point out that computer games, as we know them today, were not available when you or their parents were young. Explain that remote-controlled cars, dolls which talk, transformers and so on are also recent additions and have not always been there for children to play with.

Follow-up
• Traditional playground games are becoming more rare. Spend some time re-introducing old favourites such as 'Ring of Roses' and 'In and Out the Dusty Bluebells'.
• Invite parents/grandparents in to share rhymes, rules for playing marbles and so on. (Give plenty of notice so people have time to jog their memories.)
• Look at a reproduction poster of a painting by Pieter Bruegel the Elder called *Children's Games*. Ask the children to look carefully at the picture to discover which toys and games they recognise.

Growth

Chapter three

A topic on 'Growth' will provide many opportunities to stimulate children's wonder of life and enthusiasm for investigating what happens and why. This chapter includes a range of activities to help nurture this enthusiasm by involving children in finding out about living things and how they grow. The work also aims to help children gain a greater awareness of the need to care for plants and animals and to help them develop a respect for nature and the environment.

'Growth' and 'Change' are often entwined and this theme is explored in activities such as 'The life-cycle of a butterfly' and 'The chicken and the egg'. This work can be used to help children gain a deeper insight into the fascinating world in which we live.

Planting beans

Objective
To watch a bean grow from its first shoot to a mature plant.

What you need
Transparent jars, rectangles of thick blotting paper (the same height as the jar), beans, a jug of water, lengths of string with coloured markers at three regular intervals and a sunny window sill.

What to do
Invite the children to line the inside of their jar with blotting paper and then to pour a little water into the bottom of the jar. Each child can then carefully place their bean between the glass and the paper, so that it can be seen. Place the jars in a dark place. Let the children check their beans daily and when they begin to shoot, transfer the jars to the sunny window sill. Keep a jug of water nearby and encourage the children to keep the blotting paper moist.

An attractive effect is produced if all the jars are placed in a row along a window ledge. Tie the string around the rim of the jar and secure the other end to the top of the window. As the beans grow they will climb up the string and look like a row of Jack's beanstalks. The children can monitor growth by counting the number of markers their plant reaches.

Follow-up
• Help the children to measure the plants in metric or arbitrary units.
• Ask the children to find the biggest leaf to measure its length and width. Calculate the area of the leaf by drawing round it on squared paper and counting the number of squares covered.
• Invite the children to pick a leaf to examine the texture, shape and veins.

An imaginary beanstalk

Objective
To develop skills in simple technology.

What you need
Card tubes (from kitchen roll), wool or string, lightweight beads, card, felt-tipped pens, pencils, paints, pipe-cleaners, green fabric, green tissue, scissors, the story of 'Jack and the Beanstalk'.

What to do
Read the story of 'Jack and the Beanstalk'. Encourage the children to recall the events which lead up to Jack climbing the beanstalk. Invite the children to make an imaginary beanstalk for Jack to climb as shown in Figure 1. To do this, punch a hole near the top of a cardboard tube. Thread a length of wool through and attach a picture of Jack to the end of the wool dangling outside the tube. Thread a bead on to the end

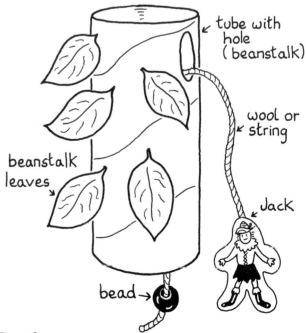

Figure 1

dangling inside and tie a knot to prevent it sliding off. Pulling down gently on the bead will make 'Jack' slowly climb up the outside of the beanstalk.

Let the children decorate their own beanstalk by colouring or painting their tube and adding paper, fabric or tissue 'leaves'. They can make 'Jack' using pipe-cleaners or by drawing his picture on card.

For safety reasons all cutting of cardboard should be done by an adult.

Follow-up
● Construct a class book called 'At the top' containing all the children's ideas about what it might be like at the top of a beanstalk. Include drawings, paintings, collages, stories and descriptions.
● Inspire 'At the top' stories by providing children with a story beginning, such as: 'When Jack got to the top of the beanstalk, he saw a face hidden in the clouds. It was . . .' or 'Jack reached the top and to his surprise he was in the land of . . .'.
● Help the children compose a zig-zag book, outlining the main sequence of events which take place either in their own stories, or in the original story of 'Jack and the Beanstalk'.

The giant's boots

Objectives
To develop practical skills in sorting, ordering and set-making. To reinforce mathematical language.

What you need
A collection of flat-heeled, clean boots and shoes in a range of sizes (include a pair of large-sized boots to be used as 'the giant's boots'), paper in a range of colours, scissors, adhesive.

What to do
Begin by letting the children have fun trying on the 'giant's boots'. Introduce the other boots and shoes to stimulate discussion about how we change in size as we grow. Encourage practical sorting and set-making tasks: ordering the shoes according to size, dividing them into groups such as 'too big for me', 'too small for me', 'the right size'.

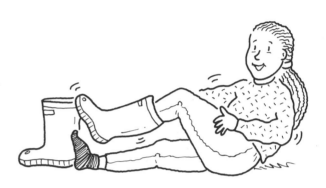

A record of this practical number work can be made by encouraging the children to draw around the sets of shoes. They can then cut and mount the 'paper soles' in pairs, sets or size order on to contrasting coloured paper. Display these on the wall or in a class book and use them to reinforce mathematical language such as 'how many', 'count the number', 'bigger than', 'smaller than', 'the same as', 'wider', 'longer'.

Follow-up
● Motivate role-play by inviting the children to make themselves a pair of giant's boots to wear before acting out the part. Rectangular tissues boxes are useful for this activity.
● Hold a 'giant boot' parade.
● Read the story *Titch* by Pat Hutchins (Picture Puffin) and talk to the children about growing too big for their clothes.
● Let the children compile a class book or photo album about how they have grown and changed.

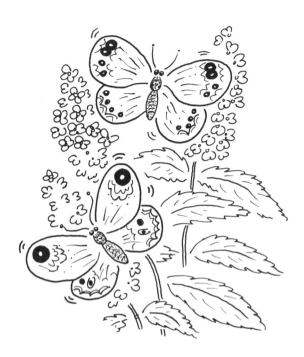

How animals change and grow

Objective
To gain an understanding of the life-cycle of a butterfly.

What you need
A safe area with plants which attract butterflies, magnifying glasses, a copy of photocopiable page 89, clipboards, paper, pencils.

What to do
Take the children on a walk to observe butterflies, caterpillars, butterfly eggs and pupae in their natural environment. Butterflies are attracted to nectar-bearing flowers such as buddleia and Michaelmus daisy. Butterfly eggs may be seen on the leaves of wild nettles. Pupae are more difficult to find as they may be hidden underneath nettle leaves which hang close to the ground.

Provide clipboards with paper and a pencil so the children can draw their findings from firsthand experience. Show the children how to use a magnifying glass to observe the intricate details on the plants and creatures. Back indoors talk to the children about how a caterpillar changes into a butterfly.

Follow-up
● Provide each child with a set of the four pictures from photocopiable page 89 and ask them to rearrange the pictures in the correct sequence to show the four main stages in the life-cycle of a butterfly.
● The children will enjoy creating butterfly prints, by adding thick paint to one side of a piece of paper and folding the paper in half. A pattern resembling butterfly wings will emerge as they unfold the paper.
● Help the children to sew or glue sequins and shiny beads on to a butterfly shape cut from felt. They can then attach pipe-cleaners as the antennae. Hang their creations to produce a colourful mobile or attach them to dowelling to make an interesting toy.

Figure 1

The chicken and the egg

Objective
To help children achieve an understanding of the changes which occur as a chick grows, both inside and outside of the egg.

What you need
Copies of photocopiable page 90, strips of card 60cm long x 10cm wide, adhesive, scissors, felt-tipped pens, coloured pencils, a chicken's egg, photographs or pictures and posters of chicks and chickens.

What to do
Explain to the children that a chicken lays eggs and incubates them by keeping them warm until they hatch into chicks. If possible, visit a local farm or zoo which houses chicks and chickens. Involve the children in making a zig-zag book (as shown in Figure 1) to reinforce their understanding of the sequence of changes which occur as a chick grows. To do this, provide each child with the set of six pictures from photocopiable page 90. Ask the children to colour these then cut them out and stick them in the correct order on to the folded strip of card. Alternatively, help the children to make a 'round about' book as shown in Figure 2. This illustrates that the process of egg, chick, chicken, egg is continuous.

Follow-up
• Talk about the things chicks need to achieve healthy growth. Basic needs are food, water, warmth, exercise and housing.
• Discuss other growth sequences in nature that are continuous, such as sunflower seeds which grow into sunflowers which produce seeds. Let the children grow a sunflower, with the aim of collecting the seeds for planting.
• Look at pips and seeds in fruit and vegetables.

Figure 2

The garden centre

Objective
To involve the children in creating a stimulating environment for imaginative play.

What you need
Tables, chairs, till, pretend money, trellis. *Items for sale:* examples of different seeds in sealed transparent bags (mustard and cress, sunflower seeds), real packets of seeds, an assortment of plain and decorative plastic flowerpots, small plants (such as a cactus), bulbs. *Imaginary flowers:* coloured tissue-paper, fine coloured fabric, coloured netting, green straws, green pipe-cleaners, adhesive, scissors, sticky tape. *Imaginary seed packets:* colourful beads, white 'window' envelopes, felt-tipped pens, coloured pencils. *Posters:* paints, felt-tipped pens, crayons.

What to do
Begin by taking the children to visit a local garden centre. Inform the parents of this work as some may be willing to organise a family trip to a garden centre.

Back in school, involve the children in setting up a structured play area based on a garden centre. Help them to arrange an interesting and imaginative display of all the items 'for sale' and let them invent an original name for their area. Help to write price tags and information labels such as 'plants for sale' and 'fill a bag with bulbs'. Encourage each child to design a seed packet for an imaginary, exotic flower. To stimulate original ideas, provide the children with a selection of coloured beads to represent the exotic 'seeds'.

Let the children use their creative skills to construct three-dimensional imaginary flowers then secure a trellis in a safe position, so that the children can use it to hang their colourful assortment of imaginary flowers and seed packets.

Encourage the children to design and paint posters of plants and flowers to include in their 'garden centre' as this will enhance the atmosphere being created. Talk about amusing situations which could occur in the garden centre and use the children's ideas to stimulate role-play. Instigate buying and selling activities to reinforce an understanding of money.

Follow-up
Grow some of the seeds sold in the garden centre. Mustard and cress are popular with young children. Show the children how to sprinkle the cress seeds on damp tissue, placed on a plastic or foil tray. Let them cover the seeds with foil and leave for three days. They can then sprinkle the mustard seeds over the tissue, cover with foil and check daily for growth to begin. When the children notice shoots showing, they should remove the foil, place their tray in a sunny position and keep the tissue moist. When the plants have grown, the children can cut the mustard and cress to eat in a sandwich.

Care for plants

Objective
To encourage an understanding of how to care for plants.

What you need
A selection of potted plants, a jug of water.

What to do
Look at the natural beauty of the plants and discuss the need to care for all living things, including plants. Share with the children ways to care for plants, such as regular watering, gentle handling and providing the correct light and environment. Let the children experience watering the plants, so that they are aware of the quantities of water needed and where to pour for best results.

Follow-up
● Invite parents to donate hyacinth bulbs that can be planted and tended by the children with the aim of holding a sale of flowering plants at a later date.
● Involve the children in creating interesting 'nooks' and 'corners' around the classroom, using plants, drapes and small collections of natural or man-made objects. Allow them to maintain these displays by giving them the responsibility of caring for the plants and collecting new artefacts to exhibit.

Roots (growing down)

Objective
To investigate root growth.

What you need
Plants such as forsythia and busy Lizzie, transparent pots, water, scissors, kitchen roll, a jug, shallow trays.

What to do
Supervise the children as they take plant cuttings. Help them look for a strong stem, then show them how to cut just below the leaf joint. The children can then place one cutting in each pot of water. Place the pots in a shallow tray lined with kitchen roll to soak up spillages. Provide a jug of water and give the children the responsibility of making sure their cuttings have water.

Encourage the children to keep a daily watch, as the roots will soon begin to grow.

Follow-up
● Help the children to make a water garden from their rooted cuttings. This can be done by lining a bowl with charcoal and adding a layer of small pebbles. The children then need to be very careful as they 'plant' their cuttings using more small pebbles to keep them upright. Keep the 'garden' watered and add a little liquid plant food each month. A beautiful display should grow and remain easy to maintain.
● Talk to the children about how the plants need water. Explain that they 'drink' water through their roots and carry it up the stem to the leaves and 'flowers'.
● Help to set up an investigation to show how plants 'drink'. Put some coloured ink in a glass of water and place a white carnation or a stick of celery in it. The children will be able to watch as the dye moves up the plant as it 'drinks' the water.

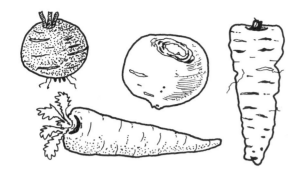

Root top garden

Objectives
To find out about root vegetables. To create a plant top garden. To observe growth.

What you need
A selection of root vegetables (carrots, parsnips, turnips, beetroot), a shallow unbreakable dish, pebbles, water, a jug, knife (for adult use only), a windowsill in the sun.

What to do
Begin by explaining how the root vegetables grow underground. If possible, arrange for the children to dig some vegetables up from a local garden or allotment. Alternatively, plan well ahead by organising a school vegetable plot.

Let the children watch as the tops are cut off the root vegetables by an adult. The children can then take over! Divide them into pairs or small groups and encourage each group to pour a little water into their dish (no more than a fingernail's depth is needed). They can then arrange the root tops from different plants in the water and place a single layer of pebbles around the tops. Place in a sunny position. The children will enjoy watching their plants grow into a lovely display, as each plant will exhibit foliage of a different texture and shade.

Follow-up
● Keep a pictorial record by asking the children to draw their garden once a week. In this way, changes and growth can be observed.
● Use the rest of the vegetables to make a vegetable soup with the children.
● Embellish the following story and use it to stimulate discussion: 'A new gardener wants to grow some carrots, so he plants the seeds, tends the ground and waters the area. He waits for a very long time, but not one nice orange carrot appears. He gets very disappointed because instead of carrots, all he gets is a mass of green weeds.

'One day, he is so fed up that he decides to pull up the nasty weeds and forget about growing carrots ever again. To his surprise, when he pulls up the green weeds he finds that the carrots are hidden underneath. They are not weeds after all, they are carrot tops!'

Food for growth

Objective
To increase the children's awareness of the foods which help us grow healthily.

What you need
Samples of real food and pictures of food.

What to do
Display the food and pictures and ask the children to talk about which foods they like best. Divide the food into two groups, one containing healthy foods (fruit and vegetables, milk, rice, beans, poultry and wholemeal bread) and those which are not so healthy when eaten in excess (sweets, cakes, biscuits). Talk to the children about how the healthy foods make our bodies grow and give us strong teeth, while too many sugary foods can make us fat and cause bad teeth.

Follow-up
• Turn your structured play area into a 'health food' shop or café.
• Make a pictorial menu booklet containing 'healthy meals' for the class café.

• Make some simple 'healthy' meals with the children, for example fruit salad.
• Record in pictures or words the sequence of events which occurred while preparing the fruit salad. Mount this on to a single sheet of paper or card, cover in sticky-backed plastic and use to develop a class recipe book.

Wholemeal rolls

Objective
To introduce children to bread making and to observe dough rising.

What you need
Ingredients: 12g dried yeast, 300ml water, 1tsp sugar, 500g wholemeal flour, 2tsps salt, 25g lard. *Utensils:* an oven, jug, large mixing bowl, large spoon, kneading board, baking tray, equipment to wash and dry hands, an apron.

What to do

Involve the children in all stages of preparation. Make sure they wash their hands before they begin.

1.   Mix the yeast, water and sugar in a jug using a spoon.
2.   Rub together the flour, salt and lard in a large bowl.
3.   Add the yeast mixture to the large bowl and mix to a dough using a large spoon.
4.   Knead the dough.
5.   Divide the dough in half and place the two pieces on a greased baking tray.
6.   Leave to stand at room temperature until the dough doubles in size.
7.   Bake in the top of the oven (200°C/400°F, gas mark 6) for 35–45 minutes.

Follow-up

• Encourage the children to recall their involvement during the preparation stages of the bread making.
• Discuss dough rising.
• Eat the bread with mustard and cress grown by the children.

Note: Bear in mind any food allergies the children may have. Some children may not be able to eat lard or animal fat – in which case vegetable fat could be used.

Stretch and grow

Objective

To have fun exploring the concept of growth, in its widest sense, through physical interpretation.

What you need

Plasticine, clay or play dough, table mats or boards, a rolling pin, aprons, facilities to wash hands.

What to do

Begin in the classroom, working with the children in small groups. Provide each child with a ball of Plasticine, clay or play dough and encourage them to manipulate their ball into a long 'snake'. While they are making it 'grow' share descriptive words with them such as: pull, roll, squash, stretch, bend and twist.

Follow-up

Follow up this activity with a movement session and remind the children of the words they used in their craft lesson. Let them interpret these words using expressive body movements.

   Focus on any three words such as stretch, roll and twist and ask the children to translate them into a short sequence of smoothly connecting movements. Encourage the children to think about a stationary pose to begin and end their sequence. Develop this theme into a dance by allowing the children to interpret their movements in time to music.

Colour

Chapter four

This chapter offers a range of activities on the theme of colour, which can be used to inspire the children's imagination and sense of investigation, such as observing coloured bubbles, finding out about colours in nature and exploring which colours can be seen easiest at night. The children will also have the opportunity of making and changing colours in a variety of activities such as mixing paints, changing the colour of lights and observing colours which change with time.

Mixing colours

Objective
To develop colour-mixing skills.

What you need
Powder paints (red, blue and yellow), brushes, a water pot, sponge (to take excess clean water off brush), mixing palette, paper.

What to do
Encourage the children to mix any two primary colours:
• red and yellow to produce orange
• red and blue to produce purple, or
• blue and yellow to produce green.
   Let the children experiment with the paint by finding out how many different types of orange, purple or green they can mix.

Follow-up
• Encourage the children to mix their own paints to create a pattern which fills the page.
• Initiate 'ongoing' paintings, that is paintings which the children can return to over a period of time adding a little more detail each session.
• Introduce white paint so that the children can create a range of shades.

Guess the flavour

Objective
To inspire an interest in investigation.

What you need
Four transparent jugs containing four different squashes (blackcurrant, orange, lemon and lime, for example), paper or plastic cups, labels, pens, food dyes.

What to do
Dilute each sample of squash and label the jugs 1–4. Draw the children's attention to the squashes and encourage them to predict the flavours by appearance alone. The numbers on the jugs can be used to identify which 'squash' the children are referring to during discussion. Let the children taste a sample to find out if their predictions were correct. Discuss the results with the children.
   Now add a little food dye to four jugs of squash to change the colours and repeat the above investigation. Let the children find out if they can still predict the flavours correctly.

Follow-up
Set up an investigation using coloured fruit sweets. Let the children investigate whether or not they can predict the flavours.

Colourful flowers

Objective
To encourage observation and creative skills.

What you need
Potted plants, a margarine tub, coloured paper and card, crayons, scissors, adhesive, sticky tape, coloured tissue-paper.

What to do
Look at the potted plants with the children. Encourage them to identify features such as leaves, stalk, petals and talk about the colours and shapes of the different parts of the plant.

Tape leaves into tub

Paper 'leaves' secured around inside edge of tub

Figure 1

Invite the children to create a three-dimensional model of a plant. First let them select their own colours for the leaves and stalk, and then encourage them to draw the shapes and cut them out. A large bright flower can then be drawn and cut out by each child and attached to their 'stalk'. Help the children to tape the leaves to the inside edge of the tub and secure the flower to the base. Brown tissue can be added as soil (see Figure 1).

Follow-up
● Discuss with the children why they chose particular colours for their 'leaves', 'stalk' and 'flower'.
● Press some flowers with the children and use them to create cards and calendars.
● Dry suitable flowers in the classroom and display them in colourful pots or vases made by the children.
● Create or enhance classroom displays using colourful drapes, potted plants and bunches of flowers.
● Go on a walk to observe colourful flowers.

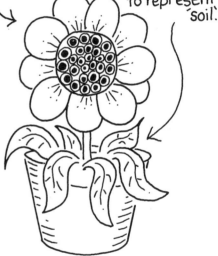

Paper flower on card 'stalk' secured to base of tub

Hide sticky tape using brown tissue paper to represent 'soil'.

Making a collection

Objective
To increase the children's awareness of the extensive existence and use of colour in everyday life.

What you need
An A4 book for each child containing approximately three or more pages, a pen.

What to do

Encourage the children to create a 'colour collection' book as an 'ongoing' activity which they can develop over a period of time. Label each page within the book with a colour and invite the children to gradually fill the book with an array of coloured samples. These can be collected at home or in school and may include: wallpaper, shiny paper, tissue-paper, card, opaque paper, fabric, wool, lace, ribbon and so on. Compare the different shades available for each colour.

Encourage the children to talk about their collection by recalling where they found their samples and why they included them.

Follow-up

● Introduce 'personal sketch books'. Encourage the children to use the book as an ongoing collection of their own drawings, designs, cuttings, patterns, ideas and so on.
● Invite the children to use their sense of colour, shade and pattern to design wallpaper for a doll's house. Use the children's work to decorate an old doll's house or to line the inside of a box to create a child-made doll's house for use in the classroom.

Changing colours

Objective

To show that colours in nature can change with time and to develop an awareness of the reasons why.

What you need

An unripe (green) tomato, an apple, a knife (for adult use only), an unripe (green/yellow) banana, a window-sill in the sun.

What to do

Children can set up a few experiments to investigate this. Some results will take longer to develop than others.
● Invite the children to leave an unripe green tomato on a sunny window-sill to ripen and turn red.
● Leave a freshly-cut apple on a plate until the white centre turns brown.
● Leave an unripe green banana on a sunny window-sill to ripen and turn yellow. Leave it longer until it overripens and brown speckles begin to appear.

Talk with the children about the changes in colour which take place.

Follow-up

Encourage the children to consider questions such as:
— How do we know when a tomato is ripe and ready to eat?
— What happens to the colour of an apple when it has been cut?

Colours in bubbles

Objective

To inspire descriptive and poetic language.

What you need

Bubble mixture, a hoop to blow bubbles with, paper and pen, coloured card, scissors.

What to do

Invite the children to have fun blowing bubbles. Encourage them to look carefully and describe the different colours that swirl around on the surface of each bubble. Extend this further by asking them to describe how the bubble moves through the air and the shapes created as the bubble is blown through the hoop.

See-through colours

Objective

To increase the children's awareness of colours and to inspire descriptive language.

Record the descriptive words used by the children on coloured circles of card or paper and use them to inspire poetic language by inviting the children to arrange the words under the heading: 'Our bubbles are . . .' For example 'Our bubbles are . . . floating . . . colourful . . . round.' Display the coloured circles on the wall, as a mobile or in a round bubble poem book.

Follow-up

● Make colourful bubble prints. Half-fill a small container (for example a yogurt pot) with a mixture of detergent and liquid paint (or mixed powder paint). Let the children use straws to blow into the mixture until the bubbles overflow. They can then be used to create a print by carefully placing a small sheet of paper against the bubbles. For more than one colour use several pots with each pot containing a different coloured mixture.
● Develop needle and thread skills by assisting the children in sewing 'bubbles' cut from brightly-coloured felt circles on to a black fabric background. Only one stitch per circle is needed, with the thread running randomly across the back of the black fabric.

What you need

Unobstructed windows, coloured Cellophane, black card or paper, coloured pens and pencils, white paper.

What to do

Secure large pieces of coloured Cellophane on to some windows at the children's eye level. Frame each colour using black card or paper. Invite each child to look through the different coloured windows and encourage them to describe what they can see.

Help the children to construct an 'I can see' book to accompany each window including pictures and writing inspired by their colourful observations.

Follow-up

● Encourage the children to investigate colour changes by looking through several layers of coloured Cellophane.
● Invite the children to make a pair of coloured 'glasses' to wear.
● Inspire original stories by asking the children to imagine a magical land where it rains coloured raindrops. Share ideas about what might happen when the raindrops touch something. What might happen if you tread in a coloured puddle?

A coloured light circuit

Objective
To develop an understanding of constructing a simple electrical circuit.

What you need
Single strand wire with plastic covering, a bulb, bulb holder, battery with screw terminals (or battery and battery holder – use a battery with a lower voltage than the bulb), small pieces of coloured tissue-paper.

What to do
Make a simple circuit with the children (as shown in Figures 1 to 4). Let them disconnect and reconnect the wires to find out what makes the light go on and off (assistance may be needed here as this can be rather 'fiddly'). Encourage the children to experiment changing the colour of the light by placing the bulb behind different coloured tissue-paper.

Follow-up
● Encourage the children to use layers of red, yellow and blue tissue-paper to create a light that is orange, green or purple.
● Invite the children to turn three circuits into a set of simple traffic lights using green, orange and red tissue-paper.

Making a simple circuit: Figures 1 and 2 should be done by an adult as part of preparation work. Figures 3 and 4 should be completed by the children with the help of the adult.

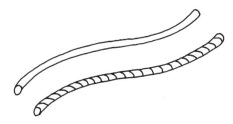

Figure 1: Cut two lengths of wire (15–20cm is sufficient).

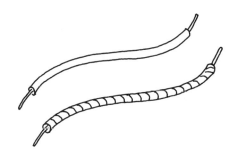

Figure 2: Remove approximately 2–3cm of plastic sheath from both ends of each length of wire.

Figure 3: Secure both wires under the screws on the bulb holder.

Figure 4: Complete the circuit by securing both wires under the screw terminals on the battery (or battery holder).

Colours at night

Objective
To increase the children's awareness of which colours are the safest to wear at night.

What you need
A large sheet of black paper, coloured sticky paper (include white, black, red, blue, green, brown, yellow, orange, purple), scissors.

What to do
Involve the children in a simple investigation to find out which colours are more easily seen at night. This activity will be most relevant to the children during the winter as they are more likely to have recent firsthand experience of dark mornings or evenings travelling to and from school.

Begin by talking with the children about the need to be seen at night, especially if they have to cross a road. Then cut the coloured sheets of paper to represent a child's coat. The size and shape of each 'coat' should be identical as the only variable in this investigation should be colour. Invite the children to stick all the 'coats' on to a large sheet of black paper to represent children walking in the dark. Now view the 'coats' from a distance (across the classroom perhaps). Which colours are easy to see? Which colours are difficult to see?

Encourage the children to draw conclusions from their investigations. Which colours do they think are the best to wear at night if you want to be seen?

Follow-up
• Provide coloured paper and fabrics, including reflective materials, for the children to make an armband to wear at night.
• Use fluorescent pens to draw people wearing armbands or emergency vehicles with fluorescent strips.

Camouflage in nature

Objective
To increase awareness of camouflage.

What you need
Pictures or photographs of animals demonstrating camouflage (moths and fish, for example), coloured paper or fabric, scissors, adhesive.

What to do
Show the children the pictures of 'camouflaged' animals and discuss camouflage in nature. Invite them to investigate which colours show up or 'disappear' against a given background.

An example of this is to use coloured paper or fabric to make a frieze of yellow 'buttercups' then to create 'butterfly' shapes from a variety of different colours to 'sit' on the buttercups. Encourage the children to say which colour butterflies become camouflaged.

Follow-up
• Challenge the children to use splatter painting to create speckled 'fish' and speckled 'sand' which show camouflage.
• Invite the children to look at minibeasts under logs and compare the colours of the tiny creatures and their surroundings.
• If possible, show the children animals which have perfected camouflage, such as stick insects and some caterpillars.

FAVOURITE COLOURS

BLUE	ORANGE	PINK	YELLOW	GREEN	RED

Recording colours

Objective
To develop skills in collecting, collating and using information in the form of graphs, bar charts and histograms.

What you need
A large sheet of paper (approximately A1) with a grid drawn on it, coloured sticky labels.

What to do
Encourage the children to help compile a class graph showing 'favourite colours'. This can be achieved by asking each child to place one coloured sticky label in the column representing their favourite colour. Alternative themes for graphs could focus on personal attributes, for example eye colour, hair colour and so on. Graphs can also be used to record popularity of coloured items (lunch boxes, shoes, jumpers and so on).

Follow-up
Use the graphs to stimulate mathematical language such as 'more than', 'less than', 'most', 'least', 'the same as', 'how many?', 'compare'.

Colour walk

Objective
To inspire an interest in nature's beauty.

What you need
An area of natural beauty within easy distance of the school — a park with trees, grass and flowers/a pond/a river/the sea shore.

What to do
Go on a walk to an area of natural beauty. Encourage the children to observe the natural colours all around them then focus their attention on to something very small, for example the head of a flower, a chipped pebble, lichen on a tree. Encourage them to look at it in detail and describe the colours they can see. During this walk, play 'Colour I Spy' with the children — 'I spy with my little eye something which is . . . blue'.

It can be surprising for children to discover how very colourful nature can be.

Follow-up
• Help the children to study the colours of plants, lichens and flowers with a magnifying glass, hand-lens or microscope.
• Encourage the children to draw or paint scenes from nature during outdoor painting sessions.
• Let the children help to set up a 'leave alone' area within the school grounds. This will encourage colourful plants such as wildflowers, weeds, shrubs and grass to become established relatively quickly.
• Let the children visit the 'wild' area regularly to observe the colours of nature, the changes which occur during each season and the type of animals which begin to settle there.

Pets

Chapter five

Caring for a pet in school provides particularly valuable experiences for young children, especially if they are fully involved in all aspects of its welfare, such as feeding, cleaning and helping to keep it secure and healthy.

However, not all schools or nurseries have the facilities to keep animals on a permanent basis. The activities in this topic are therefore not dependent upon having pets in school. Instead, it is suggested that the children benefit from regular animal visits to the school or by visiting places where animals are kept, such as pet shops, farms, bird sanctuaries and zoos. Full use can also be made of animals in the local environment, such as minibeasts, birds and local pets.

Our pet shop

Objective
To involve the children in creating a stimulating environment for imaginative play.

What you need
A pet shop within easy distance of the school, soft toy animals, baskets, cages, animal food boxes and samples of dry pet food, toys for pets, collars, leads, picture and information books about pets, a till, real or pretend money, paper, pencils, pens, a tape recorder.

What to do
If possible arrange a visit to a local pet shop. Talk about the various animals. Record the sounds they make and show the children the different types of food and cages available.

Back in school, invite the children to help set up a structured play area based on a 'pet shop'. Let them organise the toy animals into cages, or baskets, display the pet foods in tubs and write information labels such as 'open', 'closed', 'kittens for sale', 'please pay here'. The children could also paint posters about caring for animals, write messages for a 'lost and found' notice-board and design short pamphlets illustrating how the school pet is fed, or how a cage is cleaned. Play the tape-recorded animal noises in the background to enhance the atmosphere even further.

Follow-up
• Invite the children to manipulate clay or play dough into model animals — provide feathers, lolly sticks and other objects for decoration.

• Talk about the RSPCA and discuss issues such as 'caring for pets'.
• Help the children to make simple soft toy animals using felt, fur fabric or other non-fraying materials.
• Grow seeds found in hamster food, such as sunflower seeds.

A pet photoboard

Objective
To stimulate descriptive language.

What you need
A 'photoboard' or large photograph frame, photographs of pets, paper, pens, pencils.

What to do
Make a photoboard as shown in Figure 1 or use a large photograph frame. Invite the children to bring a photograph of a family pet to school. Children without a pet could use a photo of a friend's or relative's pet, or a magazine picture of a pet they would like. Each child can then slip their photographs into a 'pocket' on the photoboard.

Use the photographs as a stimulus for language work by encouraging the children to share information about the pet in their photo. They could include information such as the pet's name, age, what type of animal it is, what it eats, any endearing habits and so on.

Follow-up

• Encourage the children to write about or describe the pet in their photo. This work can then be added to the photoboard.

• Play a game entitled 'Which Pet?' by encouraging the children to take turns to describe one of the pets on the photoboard. Can the other children identify 'which pet' the description refers to?

• Let the children use a camera to take pictures of class or school pets or wild animals such as birds, squirrels and minibeasts.

• Organise a visit to a farm or zoo, or invite pets into the classroom. Encourage the children to look closely at the way the animals move and point out specific features such as whiskers, fur, claws and so on.

• Encourage the children to compare animal body parts and talk about which parts humans have in common with animals and which attributes are different.

An animal's point of view

Objectives

To increase awareness about caring for animals. To help children develop story-telling skills.

What you need

A pet in the classroom for the children to study or, alternatively, a selection of pictures and photographs of pets.

What to do

Choose a comfortable place to sit, where the children feel at ease to share their views and ideas. Ask them to imagine how a new pet feels when arriving in a new home. What would it look to for comfort? Would it miss its family? How would a new pet feel about you? Share ideas on how a pet could be made to feel happy and secure.

Follow-up

• Encourage the children to tell/write a short story called 'My pet's story' in which they imagine that their pet could explain what life is like with them. Ask questions such as 'Would your pet say you are kind?', 'Why?', 'Would your pet say that they feel happy being with you?', 'Why?'

• Ask children without pets to tell/write why an animal would like to be with them.

Figure 1

Health care – the vet

Objective
To increase the children's awareness about the role of a vet and the needs of 'injured' or 'sick' animals.

What you need
Soft toys, bandages, a stethoscope, blankets, bowls, boxes of 'food', animals' baskets and cages.

What to do
If possible, arrange for the children to visit a local vet. Encourage imaginative play by inviting the children to help set up an animal hospital or vet's surgery using toy animals. Reinforce the need to care for animals by involving the children in role-play situations which focus on helping pets that are 'injured' or 'sick'.

Follow-up
• Arrange for the children to handle a healthy animal. Stress the need to be gentle and calm so as to avoid startling them. (Be aware of any children with allergy problems.)

• Involve the children in all aspects of looking after a school or class pet by letting them feed it and clean its 'home'.
• Help the children to think about the welfare of animals in the wild by inviting them to put food out for the birds.
• Create an observation point, so the children can view the birds eating without frightening them away.

Bed for a toy animal

Objective
To help develop the children's skills in constructing three-dimensional models.

What you need
Commercial construction kits such as Lego, Mobilo or Duplo, soft toy animals, a selection of craft materials such as tubs, tubes and boxes, fabric, sponge, scissors, adhesive.

What to do
Invite the children to use their creative skills to make a three-dimensional model bed suitable for a toy animal. Encourage them to consider factors such as size and strength of the bed and how comfortable the 'bedding' feels.

Follow-up
● Discuss with the children where different pets sleep, for example in a kennel, in straw, on a perch.
● Pose questions to stimulate discussion, debate and curiosity, such as 'Does a fish go to sleep?', 'Does a horse sleep standing up?', 'Why does a budgie not fall off its perch when asleep?' Use information books to help find answers.
● Discuss with the children where wild animals sleep.

Food for pets

Objective
To help the children understand the importance of providing the correct food for pets.

What you need
A cardboard box, thick pen, scissors, a selection of pet foods including samples of dog food such as bones, biscuits, tins of meat.

What to do
Begin by reciting the rhyme 'Old Mother Hubbard' and talk about the meaning of the words 'and when she got there the cupboard was bare, and so the poor dog had none'. Use the selection of pet foods to stimulate discussion about what food should have been in the cupboard that would be suitable for the dog to eat. Talk about what would happen if the dog had nothing to eat.

Encourage the children to turn a cardboard box into Old Mother Hubbard's empty cupboard (see Figure 1) and let them have fun reinforcing their understanding by stocking the cupboard with appropriate food.

Follow-up
● Investigate what food other animals like to eat (seeds, insects, worms and so on).
● Discuss how different animals eat and drink (lapping, pecking, gnawing, chewing).
● Line up a few 'cupboards' for the children to label – 'cat food', 'hamster food', 'dog food' and so on. Encourage them to place the correct food into each 'cupboard'. Use this as an interactive display and to stimulate discussion.

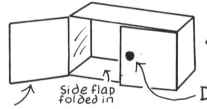

Side flap folded in

Basic cardboard box

Door handle drawn on flap

Flaps on cardboard box: used as cupboard doors.

Fill the cupboards with the correct foods.

Figure 1

Do pets have toys?

Objective
To encourage simple research and develop skills in collecting and recording information.

What you need
A copy of photocopiable page 91 for each child, pens.

What to do
Involve the children in some simple research by inviting them to find out if pets have toys. Encourage them to do this by asking friends, teachers and relatives if their pet has a toy. Let them use a copy of photocopiable page 91 to record their findings. Discuss the results with the children.

Follow-up
• Invite the children to make a toy for a kitten or puppy.
• Can the children find out if wild animals have toys?

Minibeasts

Objective
To help the children gain an interest and appreciation of tiny creatures and to develop a respect for nature.

What you need
An area outdoors which attracts 'minibeasts', for example a few logs on soil; magnifying glasses, hand-lenses, a shallow tray.

What to do
Encourage the children to observe minibeasts in their natural habitat. Initiate simple investigations to find out how many different kinds of creature can be seen and where they can be found. Provide hand-lenses and magnifying glasses so that close observations of the minibeasts and insects can be achieved *in situ*. Alternatively, small logs can be placed in a shallow container and viewed indoors.

Help the children to develop a respect for nature by encouraging them to replace the logs and their inhabitants as soon as they have finished their observations and investigations.

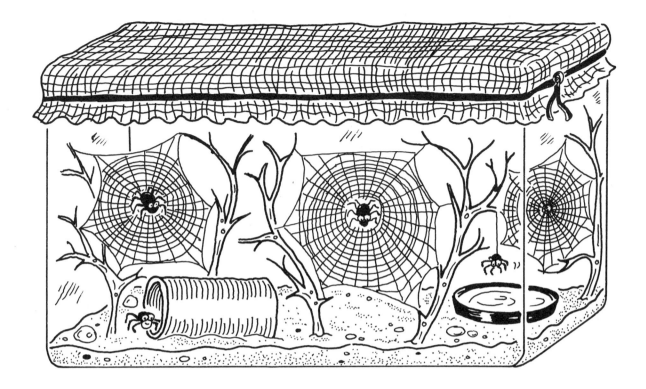

Follow-up

● Encourage the children to help construct a wormery by placing worms and soil in a transparent jar. (Take soil from a place where worms were collected and avoid heavy clay.) Add a layer of leaves or compost on the top of the soil and cover the jar with a removable 'blackout screen' such as a black paper cover. Sprinkle the soil occasionally with water to keep it moist. The children will soon be able to observe the tracks and burrows made by the worms. After about two weeks let the children help return the worms to where they were found.

● Keep spiders in transparent containers such as an empty fish tank, with fine netting secured across the top. Place a layer of soil in the base of the container and include some twigs for web support. A small tube or hollow brick should be added for shelter and a shallow dish of water should also be included to provide moisture. (The water should be renewed daily.) Keep the atmosphere moist by applying a very fine spray of water each morning. The children will enjoy watching the webs appear and observing the spiders in action. Involve the children in releasing the spiders after a few days.

Animal attributes

Objective

To encourage the children in making and playing an identification and matching game.

What you need

Two identical collections of 12 animal pictures or photographs, paints, paper, card, scissors, adhesive, story: 'Noah's Ark', song: 'The Animals Went in Two by Two'.

'Noah's Ark' painted and placed on folded card

Animals going two by two into the ark

Figure 1

What to do

Read the story of Noah's Ark to the children and sing 'The Animals Went in Two by Two' together to familiarise the children with the Noah story, then invite them to help make a game based on the story of Noah's Ark. First ask a group of children to paint a large picture of the Ark. Mount this on folded card so that it stands up. Next, encourage the children to stick the animal pictures on to pieces of folded card (24 cards in total) as shown in Figure 1.

To play

Ask four children to sit beside the 'Ark'. Share out the first collection of pictures among the group, keeping the second collection in a pile to one side. Explain to the children that the aim of the game is for their animals to join the queue to enter the Ark. To achieve this they must correctly identify their animal's matching companion by listening carefully to the clues given by you, the teacher.

Remove an animal picture card from the top of the pile, being careful not to let the children see it. Begin with simple identification such as 'Who has the animal that says meow?', 'Who has the animal with paws, whiskers and a long

tail?', 'Who has the animal with webbed feet, a beak and feathers?' When the companion is correctly identified let the child place the matching pair in the queue to enter the 'Ark'. The winner is the first child to place all of their 'animals' in the queue.

Follow-up

Encourage the children to work in pairs to paint two pictures of each animal. Mount each painting on to folded A3 card. Use the 'Ark' and the children's paintings of animals to create an interesting three-dimensional interactive display.

Young and old

Objective

To increase the children's awareness of the similarities and differences between animals and their young.

What you need

A set of pictures or photographs of baby animals, a set of pictures/photographs of the parent animals, card, scissors, adhesive.

What to do

Use the pictures to introduce names for baby animals and to initiate discussions about the similarities and differences in the appearance of animals and their young.

Let the children help to make the components for a pairing game by asking them to stick pictures of six baby animals on to each face of a die. The die can be constructed from card as shown in Figure 1. Pictures of the parent animal should be mounted separately on to six sheets of card.

To play
Place the pictures of the adult animals face up. Let the children take turns to throw the die to reveal a baby animal. If, say, a piglet is shown, the player must select and keep the card showing the mother pig. Give the children plenty of clues and encouragement to help them choose the correct card.

Figure 1

Follow-up

An alternative game can be played. Lay the pictures of the parent animals face down. Let the children take it in turns to throw the die. If, say, a piglet is shown, the player must turn over a card showing the parent animal – if it illustrates a pig, the player keeps the card, if not, the card should be replaced face down. The next player repeats the process. The winner is the player who has collected most cards.

Animals which help us

Objective

To develop the children's respect and understanding of guide dogs.

What you need

A guide dog with owner, a blindfold, 'obstacles'.

What to do

Discuss animals that help us with the children, such as guide dogs, sheep dogs and police dogs. If possible, arrange for a blind person and their guide dog to visit the class. Invite the children to play a game to help them understand how important a guide dog is to someone who cannot see. Do this by placing a few 'obstacles' on the floor. Then, with the children working in pairs, let them take it in turn to lead their blindfolded partner around the obstacles.

Follow-up

Ask the children to imagine how they would have felt, while blindfolded if their 'guide' had not been there to help them negotiate the obstacles.

Relate this to how a blind person may feel if they have no guide dog to help them.

Unusual pets

Objective
To encourage the children to make decisions and increase their skills in 'set' making.

What you need
PE hoops, pictures or photographs of: pets, farm animals, wild animals and animals from other countries (include some pictures of unusual pets such as snakes and tarantulas).

What to do
Encourage the children to sort the pictures into two 'sets', one illustrating the animals they consider would make good pets to have in their own home the other for animals which would not make good pets. Let the children use two large PE hoops to contain each 'set' and stimulate discussion about the reasons for their decision. The children will be fascinated to hear about some of the unusual pets people own, such as snakes and tarantulas. Explain that special care and equipment is essential so that these animals do not suffer.

Follow-up
• Stimulate the children's imagination and sense of the ridiculous by asking them to imagine having a pet hippo, giraffe or kangaroo in their house! Let them tell you their views on the idea!
• Encourage the children to put the animals' interests first when deciding why they would make unsuitable pets. Do this by asking the children to think about the special needs of the different animals.

Imaginary pets

Objective
To encourage the children to use their imagination.

What you need
Paper, pens, pencils, crayons or paints, pictures of real animals.

What to do
Invite the children to use coloured pens, crayons or paints to create a picture of an imaginary pet.

Use the pictures of real animals to help the children think about different animal attributes. Stimulate their imagination further by asking questions such as: 'Is your 'pet' going to have a long neck like a giraffe, or a wide neck like an elephant?', 'Will it have a beak, teeth or both?', 'If it is going to have a tail, will it help it to hang from trees like a monkey's tail, will it wag like a dog's or help it to swim like a fish's tail?', 'What type of body would you like to give to your imaginary 'pet'?, 'Will it be slimy, furry or covered in a shell?', 'Will the ears point up, flop down or be positioned on the animal's legs like a grasshopper's ears?' Use the questions to motivate discussion and to inspire the children to share ideas.

Follow-up
• Encourage the children to describe the appearance of their imaginary pet.
• Stimulate their imagination further by asking what such an animal would eat and drink. Where would it live? Would it be friendly?
• Ask the children to imagine how their pet would move. Would it scurry and scamper like a mouse, jump, bound and run like a dog or lumber like a walrus.
• Turn a programmable toy such as 'Valiant Roamer' into an 'imaginary pet'.

Shape

Chapter six

A topic on 'Shape' will initiate a lasting curiosity of the natural and the man-made world. The environment created within the nursery or classroom can be developed to entice children into looking more closely at their surroundings and help to create an interest for discovering hidden detail.

The first group of activities in this chapter can be used to develop skills in sorting and naming and to increase the children's awareness of natural and man-made shapes. Opportunities are also provided for pattern-making and observing symmetry. The activities then focus on finding out about three-dimensional shapes, stimulating a sense of investigation and how shape affects the perception of capacity.

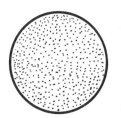  

A sorting and naming game

Objective
To introduce mathematical terms and language with regard to shape.

What you need
Card, a variety of shapes cut from sticky paper, paper, scissors, adhesive, pens, a die (with a different shape drawn on each face).

What to do
Make a die from card and draw a different shape on each face. Provide each child with an assortment of these shapes cut from sticky paper and a sheet of paper with a large circle drawn in the centre. The number and types of shape used will depend on the age and ability of the children. Invite the children to play the following game to turn their circle into a 'monster's face' using the assortment of shapes to represent its eyes, nose, mouth, hair and so on.

How to play
The first player throws the die. If, say, a triangle is thrown, that child should select a triangle from their own assortment of shapes and place it on their circle. The players continue to take turns to throw the die. If the die indicates a shape which is not available, that player misses their turn. The winner is the first player to use up all of their shapes to create a

'monster's face' inside their circle. During the game talk with the children about the names of the shapes and encourage them to identify shapes with three sides, four sides, five sides and so on.

Follow-up
Reinforce understanding of shape by providing each child with a copy of photocopiable page 92 for the following tasks:
— identifying the name of each shape;
— counting the number of different shapes;
— talking about the size differences of the triangles and finding out that the name does not alter according to the size or position of the shape.

Tallying

Objective
To increase awareness of shapes in the environment.

What you need
Pens, paper, a clipboard (optional), a room indoors.

What to do
Encourage the children to look at different shapes in the classroom or nursery, for example the shape of the windows and doors. Invite them to investigate how many of these everyday objects are round, square, oblong, hexagonal or triangular and to record their observations by keeping a tally of each shape as it is seen. Ask the children which shapes were seen most often and which shapes were rarely seen.

Follow-up

• Go on a local walk to observe the different shaped windows and doors on houses and shops. If possible, keep a tally of these different shapes. Back in the classroom, discuss which shapes were common and which shapes were rare.
• Encourage the children to construct a two-dimensional or three-dimensional house, shop, church or other building with windows and doors which flap open, and closed. Let the children select their own shape for these 'flaps'.
• Visit a local church to observe the unusual shapes of the windows and doors. Look at the shapes and designs on the stained glass windows.

Stained glass windows

Objective

To appreciate the aesthetic possibilities of shape.

What you need

Black paper or card, scissors, coloured tissue-paper or fine fabric, adhesive or sticky tape, photographs or pictures of stained glass windows, a church/building with real stained glass windows.

What to do

Show the children an example of a stained glass window (a church, house porch or shop front) or, if this is not feasible, use photographs or pictures.

Encourage the children to make their own representation of a stained glass window by folding over the four corners on a sheet of black paper or card and then cutting a shape of their choice out of each fold as shown in Figure 1 (keep these for the follow-up). Next, ask them to unfold the corners and secure coloured tissue or fine fabric over the reverse side of each 'hole'.

Every child's 'stained glass window' will be unique in design, which can create a colourful effect when placed against a real window.

Follow-up

• Encourage the children to look closely at the folded shapes cut from their sheet of black paper. Talk about symmetry, point out that the fold down the centre of their shape is the line of symmetry.
• Invite the children to look at shapes in patterns such as the patterns used during some religious festivals, for example rangoli patterns and the mehndi patterns drawn on the back of hands.

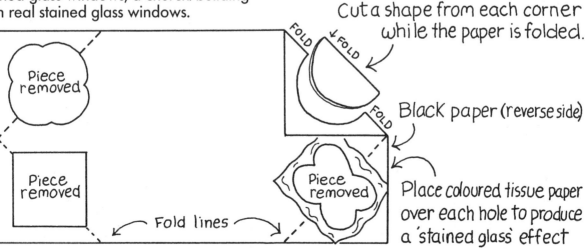

Cut a shape from each corner while the paper is folded.

Black paper (reverse side)

Place coloured tissue paper over each hole to produce a 'stained glass' effect

Figure 1

Looking at honeycomb

Objective
To gain a greater awareness of shapes in nature.

What you need
A real honeycomb, reference books about bees, a bee-keeper (if possible).

What to do
Invite the children visually to examine the honeycomb. Talk with them about the shape of each individual cell made by the bees and the pattern created when many cells are grouped together. Introduce words such as 'hexagon' and 'tessellate'. If possible, invite a local bee-keeper to talk to the children or use information books and picture books to help them gain a greater understanding of bees and honeycombs.

Follow-up
• Encourage the children to count the number of sides on a two-dimensional hexagonal shape.
• Provide six or more two-dimensional hexagons of the same size, so the children can fit them together, jigsaw style, to represent a honeycomb pattern.
• Invite the children to make honey sandwiches.

• Use hexagonal-shaped sponges to print tessellating patterns on to fabric or paper.
• Help the children to sew hexagonal pieces of fabric together to form a class patchwork. (The simplest method is to help the children attach the patches on to a larger sheet of plain fabric, using a single cross-stitch in the centre of each hexagon.)

Inside fruit and vegetables

Objective
To encourage the children to use descriptive language.

What you need
A selection of fruit and vegetables which have an interesting cross-section (kiwi fruit, oranges, lemons, grapefruit, tomato, red cabbage), a knife (for adult use only), a large tray, kitchen roll.

What to do
Let the children feel and compare the shape of the fruit and vegetables. Encourage them to describe the shapes from visual and tactile observation. Cut the fruit and vegetables in half and display them on a tray lined with kitchen roll. Let the children look at and talk about the shapes and patterns inside the fruit and vegetables. Talk about the symmetry of the cross-section of the fruit.

Follow-up
• Invite the children to complete observational drawings of the fruit and vegetables.
• If the fruit has not been handled or left for long, let the children help make a fruit salad.

Leaves collage

Objective
To investigate symmetry.

What you need
A collection of leaves which are different shapes and sizes, adhesive, card, small mirrors.

What to do
Encourage the children to compare the different shapes of the leaves and invite them to make a leaf collage.

Stimulate the children's imagination by suggesting that they use the leaves to represent the shapes of flowers, animals or birds. Alternatively, they could design their own leaf patterns. Cover the children's work with a sheet of transparent sticky-backed plastic to help protect the leaves.

Let the children use small mirrors to investigate the symmetry of the individual leaves in their collage. They can also have fun finding out if their leaf picture is symmetrical.

Follow-up
● Invite the children to use the leaves to design and make their own, original greeting cards.
● Let the children observe other symmetrical objects in the natural environment, for example feathers, butterflies and the human body.

● Invite the children to create a 'symmetrical garden' by securing two small mirrors at right angles on to the inside edges of a small box. Cut away the other two sides and let the children fill the base with shells, stones, small leaves, flower heads and so on. The mirror will create an illusion of a 'garden' which is symmetrical in two directions.

Body shapes

Objective
To develop an awareness of body shapes.

What you need
A room with enough space to move around freely and safely, a tape recorder and music suitable for movement activities.

What to do
Begin by encouraging the children to use their whole body to investigate making symmetrical shapes, such as 'star' shapes and 'pin rolls' and non-symmetrical shapes such as 'twisted', 'curly' or 'pointed' shapes. Develop this theme by asking the children to move from one shape to another (from a symmetrical shape to one which is non-symmetrical). Encourage them to do this using slow, controlled movements, or suddenly in response to a sound or signal. Then, encourage the children to explore 'moving shapes' such as 'twirling' or 'spinning'.

Extend the theme further by introducing music. The children can work individually, in pairs or in groups to create short dance sequences based on changing shapes and moving shapes.

A tube rocket

Objective
To develop skills in construction using three-dimensional shapes.

What you need
A wide selection of different-sized tubes and boxes, adhesive, card, models of toy rockets, pictures of real rockets, wool, fabric, netting.

What to do
Invite the children to look at pictures and models of rockets and talk with them about the shapes of the different parts of the rocket. Introduce words such as 'cone', 'tube', 'cylinder', 'cube', 'block'.

Let the children sort through the tubes and boxes to identify shapes which they could use to create a model of a rocket. Encourage a high degree of independence as the children construct their model. When complete, help the children to secure a length of wool to the top of their 'rocket'. This can then be threaded through a piece of fabric or netting and attached to the wall or ceiling. When the thread is pulled the 'rocket' takes off.

Follow-up
● Let the children 'fly' their rockets to stimulate their imagination as to the noise their own rocket might make if it were able to 'take off'. Encourage them to translate these sounds into words, such as 'zoom', 'rumble', 'roar'.
● Display the rockets and words on the wall or as mobiles.
● Use a large roll of corrugated card to turn the home corner into a rocket.
● Invite the children to make their own 'helmets' to wear in their 'rocket' by folding, rolling or bending a flat sheet of card into a three-dimensional shape.
● Encourage the children to look out for cylinders and cones in their everyday environment (post boxes, pencil pots, biscuit tins).

Kites of different shapes

Objective
To encourage observation and inspire confidence in practical design.

What you need
Examples of commercial kites in different shapes and sizes (if possible include two-dimensional and three-dimensional kites), lightweight paper and fabric, straws, wool, string, ribbon, sticky tape, adhesive, pens.

What to do

Invite the children to have a close look at the commercial kites by focusing their attention on the different shapes used to make the kites. If possible, arrange for extra adult helpers, so the children can experience flying the kites.

Back in the classroom, encourage the children to construct a kite of their own, using lightweight materials. Encourage each child to use practical trial and error to discover kite shapes and designs which appeal to them. Let the children test their kite designs outside by holding on to the kite string and running to see if their kite flutters above the ground behind them.

Follow-up

● Ask the children what they think it would feel like to be taken up with their kite. Stimulate their imagination by telling a short story. The following is an example that can be adapted or extended:

'One windy day some children were flying their kites on the top of a high hill. The youngest and smallest child, Jack, was holding the largest and strongest kite. It was his favourite birthday present and Jack wanted to fly it all by himself.

'But, the wind began to get stronger and the kite was tugging harder. Suddenly a huge gust of wind blew Jack off the ground and up into the air with the kite. The youngster held on tight to the kite's string as they flew up higher and higher. Jack looked down and saw . . .'

Talk with the children about what Jack might have seen. Where might his kite have taken him and how might he have landed?

● Provide some aerial photographs for the children to look at. Let them have fun identifying features such as houses, roads and fields.

Shapes in clay

Objective
To experience creating irregular shapes in clay.

What you need
Soft manageable clay, clayboards, tools to create texture (old forks, a comb, sponge, sieve, blunt knife), aprons, artefacts which are interesting and irregular in shape (driftwood, large smooth stones, ragged rock, a misshapen carrot or potato).

What to do
Invite the children to handle the artefacts and then compare shapes and textures. Provide each child with a block of clay and a board to work on. Invite them to manipulate their whole piece of clay to form a new and unusual shape. This could be, for example, curved or angular in shape, rough or smooth in texture or a combination of these. Encourage the children to make their own decisions.

Follow-up
• When all the 'sculptures' are dry, encourage the children to feel them with their eyes closed.
• Invite the children to identify everyday objects while wearing a blindfold.
• Encourage awareness of the blind and talk about Braille/textured pavements — specially textured paving to warn a blind person when they are approaching a crossing.

Guess the parcels

Objective
To motivate discussion, deliberation and decision-making.

What you need
Approximately six familiar objects (such as a sock, ball, pencil, spade) wrapping paper, sticky tape.

What to do
Wrap the objects individually making sure that, as far as possible, they still resemble the shape of the item, for example a sock should not be rolled or folded. Choose one of the objects to serve as a 'mystery parcel' which, when wrapped, is not easily recognised. Then make a feature out of displaying these 'parcels' to capture the children's interest and attention.

Encourage them to make visual and tactile observations of the parcels and to discuss thoughts and ideas as to the contents of each package. After they have had a chance to do this, let the children help unwrap each parcel to find out if their predictions were correct. Enjoy a light-hearted end to the activity by saving the 'mystery' parcel until last.

Follow-up
• Invite the children to play a 'shadow sheet' game by placing a selection of everyday three-dimensional objects on a table and covering them with a cloth. Can the children feel under or over the fabric cover to identify the objects?
• Encourage the children to make a small 'gift' for someone special (a handwritten note, a piece of sewing, a clay model). Encourage them to wrap it carefully or to select a box for it, of a suitable shape and size.

Wheels

Chapter seven

A topic on 'Wheels' can inspire the children's sense of exploration and develop their appreciation of familiar objects. The activities in this chapter aim to harness this appreciation by involving the children in discovering the different uses for wheels and their frequent occurrence in everyday life.

Through construction and investigation the children can find out how movement is affected by the shape of a wheel and by the position of its axle. The practical activities aim to show how important wheels are in making movement easier and to give firsthand experience of making simple models which travel or spin. Activities are also included to help children gain a greater understanding of other wheels, such as cogs and pulley wheels. Overall, the classroom or nursery can be turned into a hive of interesting things 'on the move'.

Wheels within wheels

Objective
To stimulate descriptive language.

What you need
A wide selection of different-sized wheels or pictures of wheels from bicycles, prams, toys, cars and so on.

What to do
Display the wheels, so that the children can look at and touch them safely. Talk about the different wheels and encourage the children to think about why some wheels are bigger than others. Explain the different attributes of the wheels and introduce words such as 'spoke', 'tyre' and 'tread'. Play a game with the children by letting them take turns to describe one of the wheels on display. Encourage other members of the group to identify the correct wheel by listening carefully to the descriptions.

Follow-up
● Rotate one or more of the wheels to stimulate the use of descriptive words such as 'turning', 'spinning', 'whizzing'. As the wheels slow down, words such as 'wobbling' may be appropriate. Use the collection of words to create simple poems, such as 'turn wheel turn, spin wheel spin'.
● Compile a wall frieze using the children's paintings of different modes of transport. Place their pictures on a 'road' and have all vehicles in the background facing in one direction while vehicles in the foreground should face the opposite direction. A striking three-dimensional effect can be achieved by mounting the pictures in the foreground on boxes to raise them away from the wall.
● Display a bicycle in the classroom so the children can study what happens when the pedals are turned, or the wheels are spun. Remind the children of the dangers of the moving parts.
● Invite the children to look closely at how the brakes work on a bicycle. Encourage them to discuss why bikes and cars need brakes.

Tyre rubbings and prints

Objective
To develop creative skills.

What you need
A selection of clean wheels with a discernable tread. *For rubbings:* white and coloured paper (approximate size 15cm square), thick coloured or metallic wax crayons with the paper removed, foil, adhesive. *For prints:* newspaper, powder paint, paper, brushes, sponges, a bowl of water, cleaning rags, aprons.

What to do
Talk about the patterns and shapes on the tyres and invite the children to take rubbings and prints. Encourage them to be creative by demonstrating a variety of techniques to experiment with. Below are some suggestions.

Rubbings
● Place the paper on the tyre and rub over the paper using the side of a crayon. Repeat the process by moving the paper slightly and rubbing with a different coloured crayon. Fill the page with rubbings.
● Place a piece of foil on the tyre and rub with the fingers until the pattern appears. Stick the foil on to a black background.

Prints
● Lay the wheels on newspaper to protect the table or floor. Brush some paint over the tread and press the paper on to the paint. The paper can then be carefully peeled away from the tyre, to reveal the print.
● Make wheel tracks by placing a paint-filled sponge on the ground, next to a large sheet of paper. The children can then push their wheeled vehicles so that the wheels roll over the paint and on to the paper.
   Do this activity outdoors. Provide water and rags to clean the wheels and do not allow children to ride through the paint as the tyres may become slippery.

Follow-up
● A wheel with spokes can be used as a stimulus for creating imaginative mobiles. Help the children to make and decorate a range of small 'spokes' using straws, pipe-cleaners or strips of card. Hang these shapes around a hoop or 'cartwheel' cut from stiff card.
● Show the children how to transform circles of card into spirals, hoops and cones. Use fine thread to hang these shapes one under the other.

Wheeled vehicle survey

Objective
To involve the children in simple investigation and go on to explore the results.

What you need
Clipboards, copies of photocopiable page 93, pencils.

What to do
Take a small group of children outdoors where they can view traffic and pedestrians from a position of safety. Encourage them to identify cars, buses, milk floats, motorbikes, bicycles and other vehicles then involve them in a simple investigation to find out how many different types of wheeled vehicle they can see. Provide each child with a clipboard and a copy of photocopiable page 93. Ask them to record what they see by placing a tick underneath the appropriate picture. Back in the classroom, discuss the results of the investigation with the children by encouraging them to use their record sheet to recall their observations.

Follow-up
• Extend the investigation by asking the children to keep a tally of the number of vehicles seen.
• Help the children to compile a class bar graph/chart to show how many buses, cars, and so on, were seen.
• Stimulate imaginative play by arranging classroom chairs to represent the seats on a bus. Provide a hat, jacket and 'steering wheel' so that the children can take turns to dress up as the driver. 'Tickets', a bell and 'money' can be used by the 'conductor'.

Make a road layout

Objective
To increase awareness of the safe use of traffic signals and to encourage co-operation.

What you need
Toys with wheels (tricycles, scooters and pedal cars). A playground or large room indoors. *Dressing up clothes:* a white shirt, reflective armbands, hard hat, police officer's outfit. *Traffic signs:* broom handles, stiff card, paints, scissors, strong adhesive tape. *Garage:* large boxes, vacuum cleaner hoses, paints, scissors.

What to do
Carefully plan a safe, well-supervised walk for the children to observe road signs and traffic signals. Afterwards, in school or nursery, discuss the children's observations and use these to reinforce their awareness of road safety and to inspire them to make a road layout of their own. Traffic signs — 'stop/go', 'keep left', 'one way', 'no overtaking', 'road works', a 'lollipop person's sign' — can be painted on to card and secured to broomsticks. A petrol pump for a garage can be made by placing a vacuum cleaner hose through a hole in the side of a large cardboard box.

Let the children take turns to act the parts of 'drivers', 'lollipop person', 'road worker', 'police traffic officer' and 'petrol pump attendant'. Ask the children to position themselves around a large circular route and invite the 'drivers' to complete the route. Emphasise the need to look out for the road signs and abide by a few 'rules of the road' such as 'keep left' and 'one way'.

Follow-up
● Extend this activity by giving the 'drivers' a job to do *en route*, such as posting a letter, taking teddy to school or delivering a parcel to the garage.
● Set up a 'pedestrian crossing' using masking tape or chalk on the floor and use the wheeled toys to represent traffic. Let the children take turns to use the crossing. Highlight the need to look, listen and be patient.

The wheels on the bus

Objective
To involve the children in making and playing a number game.

What you need
Four sheets of card or paper, each a different colour (size A1 or 85 x 60cm), 16 sheets of white card or paper (25 x 18cm), eight circular sheets of black card or paper (25cm in diameter), two wooden bricks, sticky labels, paints, felt-tipped pens.

What to do
Sing the song 'The Wheels on the Bus Go Round and Round' and invite the children to help make a game based on the song. To do this, draw the outline of a bus with four windows and two wheels on each sheet of coloured paper. Encourage the children to number the shapes 1–6 as shown in Figure 1. Provide them with the sheets of white paper or card and explain that these will be the windows on the bus. Ask the children to paint or

crayon a face looking out of the window. Some children may want to paint their own portrait or that of a friend, parent or grandparent.

Let the children help to make two dice, one showing numbers 1–6, the second showing the four bus colours, plus two white sides. The dice can be made from wooden bricks with coloured or numbered sticky labels attached to each side.

How to play
Two to twelve children can play. The four buses are placed on the floor and the children sit in a circle around the buses. The eight 'wheels' and sixteen 'windows' are shared out among the children. The first child throws both dice. If, say, a red side is shown on the first die and the number 3 on the second, the player should place a window on the red bus in frame 3. If the number die shows a 5 or 6, the child should match a wheel instead of a window to the appropriate coloured bus. If the colour die shows white, the child is allowed to throw that die again. The aim of the game is to complete all of the buses.

Figure 1

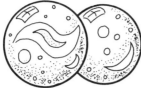

Rolling around

Objective
To encourage the children to draw conclusions from their own sets of results and to increase their awareness of three-dimensional shapes.

What you need
A selection of objects, some which will roll, such as a ball, a marble, an orange; others which will not roll, such as a book, a teddy, a key; and objects which will roll if positioned in a certain way, such as a reel of sticky tape, a bottle, a circular margarine tub.

What to do
Provide the children with the complete collection of objects and invite them to experiment to find out which ones roll and which do not roll. They can do this by pushing the objects along a flat surface or by releasing them from the top of a small slope and then group the objects accordingly. Ask the children to compare the two groups of objects and see if they can discover a third group (those objects which only roll if positioned in a certain way). Encourage the children to explain what they discovered and to draw conclusions from their results.

Follow-up
• Develop the theme of 'rolling' during PE by inviting the children to explore the different ways of rolling their bodies.
• Play team games using hoops, balls and skittles.

Models with wheels

Objective
To develop skills in design and technology.

What you need
Assorted boxes, plastic trays and containers, dowelling or garden cane, card, scissors, adhesive, wheels (or materials to make them such as cotton reels and sponge balls), thread or string, hole punch, Plasticine, elastic bands, plastic tubing, strong sticky tape, coloured sticky paper, paints.

What to do
Read *Mr Gumpy's Motor Car* by John Burningham (Picture Puffin) or one of the 'Gumdrop' books by Val Biro (Hodder & Stoughton). Invite the children to design and make a wheeled vehicle to carry a light passenger, such as a small teddy or Lego figure. Some children may need advice on how to include wheels which move freely. The examples given in Figures 1–3 can be used, or adapted, according to the individual models created by the children.

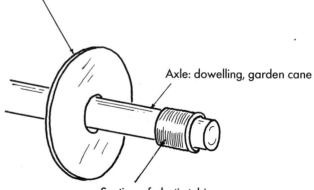

Main wheel: card, cotton reel, sponge ball, etc

Axle: dowelling, garden cane

Section of plastic tubing
(Make sure it fits 'snuggly' over dowelling.)

Figure 1

Follow-up
● Encourage the children to test the distance their model will travel and its speed when pushed across the floor or when released from the top of a slope.
● Help the children to investigate how the speed, or distance travelled, alters when more 'passengers' are added to their models.
● Let the children test their models along different types of floor surface. Discuss the results and make comparisons.
● Invite the children to attach string to their model so that it can be pulled along.

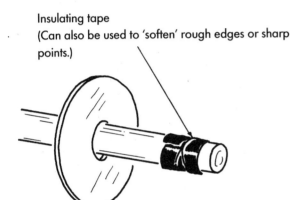

Insulating tape
(Can also be used to 'soften' rough edges or sharp points.)

Figure 2

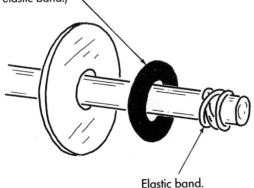

Card mini-wheel
(This prevents the main wheel from rubbing against the elastic band.)

Elastic band.

Figure 3

Different-shaped wheels

Objective
To demonstrate the need for wheels to be round in shape.

What you need
Wheeled vehicles made by the children (see preceding activity), a selection of materials which can be used as different-shaped wheels or shapes cut from thick card with a hole in the centre for the axle.

What to do
Invite the children to look at different wheels in the school or nursery (trolley wheels, wheels on bookcases, wheels under PE equipment, the piano or television). Talk with the children about the shape of all the wheels seen. Use their observations to stimulate the children's curiosity about how wheels of different shapes would perform and challenge them to find out if their model would move better with wheels of a different shape. Encourage the children to swap the round wheels on their model with items which are square, triangular, oval and so on.

Discuss the results of the tests with the children and encourage them to evaluate what happens and why.

Follow-up

- Talk with the children about the names of the various shapes. Encourage them to count the number of sides and edges on these shapes.
- Use the models with unusual-shaped 'wheels' to inspire the children's imagination for creating stories. The ideas below can be used as story beginnings. Encourage the children to make up a 'middle' and 'ending'.

'One day a clown bought a car. He had great fun driving it, but nobody else would ride with him because . . .'

'The happy clown jumped into his car, but oh dear, the wheel had fallen off! So he decided to repair it himself using . . .'

Keep a record of the children's stories for use in the book corner. These could be written using emergent writing, or illustrated to form a storyboard. Some children will enjoy watching as an adult scribes for them, while others will feel more comfortable recording their ideas on to tape. A tape recorder could also be used to capture spontaneous, or group stories told by the children.

Axles in different places

Objective
To discover how the position of the axle affects the movement of wheeled models.

What you need
Toy cars, children's models of wheeled vehicles, stiff card, a hole punch, dowelling, scissors.

What to do
Use the toy cars and children's models to explain that wheeled vehicles rest on axles and that the axle is placed in the centre of the wheel to give a steady ride. Make a model axle with wheels attached as in Figure 1 to reinforce understanding. Invite the children to remove the dowelling from the centre of the wheel and reposition it. Let them roll the axle to find out what happens to the movement.

Encourage the children to test what happens to their own models when the axles are not positioned in the centre of the wheels.

Follow-up
● Ask the children to imagine what it would feel like to be riding in a car, when the axles are not positioned in the centre of the wheels. Use the children's models to stimulate ideas and descriptions.
● Ask the children to mime a ride in a car with unusual-shaped wheels or with an axle which is off-centre.
● Develop this theme by asking the children to work in twos or fours — one child mimes the actions of the 'driver' while the other children pretend to be his passengers.

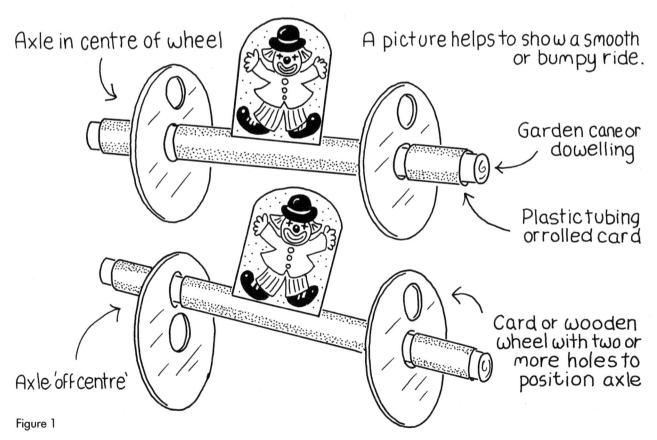

Axle in centre of wheel

A picture helps to show a smooth or bumpy ride.

Garden cane or dowelling

Plastic tubing or rolled card

Axle 'off centre'

Card or wooden wheel with two or more holes to position axle

Figure 1

73

Moving without wheels

Objective
To find out how wheels facilitate movement.

What you need
A fairly heavy box, broom handles or sticks which can be used as rollers.

What to do
Ask the children to try moving the box and then challenge them to think of a way to make it easier to move. Provide sticks as a clue. Let the children experiment with moving the box by placing the rollers underneath, allowing them to work out how best to position the rollers.

Follow-up
Divide the children into groups of three or four to play team games which involve moving boxes on rollers or wheels.
— One game involves each team moving an empty box across a room, collecting some bulky objects on the way, then if wheels are not present, using rollers on the return journey. The team to arrive back first wins the game.

— Another game requires each team to begin at one end of the room with a box containing three large (or relatively heavy) objects. The objects must be removed, one at a time, at three different 'unloading stations'. The first team to reach the opposite side of the room with an empty box is the winner.

Teddy's lift

Objective
To develop an awareness of pulley wheels.

What you need
Cotton reels, string, wool, a small teddy or doll, lightweight plastic or paper container, coat peg or hook.

What to do
Explain to the children that pulley wheels help to pull objects up or let objects down. Use commercial construction kits such as Lego or Meccano, or toy cranes to show them how pulley wheels work.
   Invite the children to make a lift for teddy using a simple pulley wheel, see Figure 1. Help them to thread a piece of string through a cotton reel and tie it to form a loop. Then tie a piece of wool to a small pot which can be used to hold teddy. When the cotton reel is hung over a hook and the wool is draped over the cotton reel, the pot containing teddy can be pulled up or lowered down by the children.

Follow-up
• Let the children have fun lifting objects other than teddy.
• Ask the children to find out what happens if they pull teddy up too fast, or let go of the wool while teddy is at the top of the pulley.

• Help the children to collect pictures of machines which lift people or objects up, such as cranes, car-recovery vehicles, scaffolding pulleys on building sites and elevators.

• Invite the children to make a crane by swapping teddy's 'basket' on the pulley for a small curtain hook. They can then lift a variety of objects.

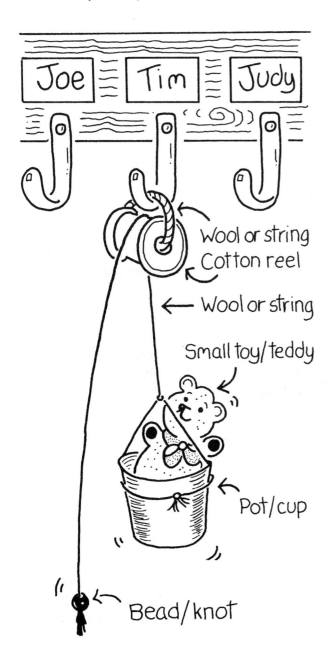

Figure 1

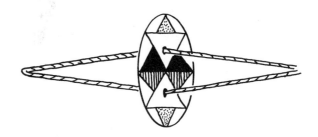

Coloured wheels

Objective
To experience the merging of colours and patterns by spinning.

What you need
Circles cut from card (approximately 10–20cms in diameter) with two small holes in the centre, felt-tipped pens, crayons and coloured pencils, strong thread such as wool or string.

What to do
Give each child a circle of card and invite them to colour both sides. Encourage them to design a bold and bright pattern using three or more colours. Help the children to thread a length of string or wool through the two holes in the centre of the card and tie this to form a loop. Position the card circle in the middle of the loop of string and, when pulled at either end, the loop can be used to spin the card disc.

Let the children spin their colour wheel and encourage each child to explain, in their own words, what they see happening to the colours.

Follow-up
• Arrange for the children to view other wheels which spin or turn, such as water wheels, windmills or spinning wheels.
• Let the children have fun playing with toys which spin and turn, such as yo-yos and spinning tops.

Clocks and watches

Objective
To inspire close observation and attention to detail.

What you need
Wind-up clocks and watches, a broken clock.

What to do
Show the children the detailed mechanism of a wind-up clock or watch. Let them observe the wheels and cogs move slowly or spin round fast. Invite the children to look inside a large clock, as this will enable them to see the cogs clearly. Point out how one cog affects another. Explain to the children how the cogs and wheels help to make the hands go round at exactly the right speed.

Dismantle an old or broken clock for the children to handle and observe the different parts closely.

Follow-up
● Use the dismantled clock to stimulate the children's interest in close observational drawing. Chalk drawings on black paper produce an interesting result.
● Read *Clocks and more clocks* by Pat Hutchins (Picture Puffin).
● A lovely display can be achieved by sticking a variety of the children's brightly-painted cogs on to a black background. Small cog shapes can be printed using cotton reels and larger cogs made by using a repeated circle of hand prints.

Nursery rhymes

Chapter eight

Nursery rhymes provide an ideal environment to stimulate children's imagination. This topic can also be used to develop an interest in a wide range of activities, some of which require quiet concentration, such as sewing a soft toy or making jewellery, while others make use of the children's enthusiasm, for example: following a crooked route, 'riding' a hobby horse or dancing like a 'crooked cat'! Other activities, however, can be used to promote consideration for others, for example: discussing how to help someone who has fallen over, or compiling a first aid kit.

There was a crooked man

There was a crooked man,
    And he walked a crooked mile,
He found a crooked sixpence
    Against a crooked stile;
He bought a crooked cat,
    Which caught a crooked mouse,
And they all lived together
    In a little crooked house.

Spot the difference

Objective
To stimulate the children's interest in the nursery rhyme and motivate discussion and observation.

What you need
A copy of the rhyme 'There was a crooked man', a copy of photocopiable page 94 for each child, coloured pencils, crayons or felt-tipped pens.

What to do
Say the rhyme 'There was a crooked man' together. Provide each child with a copy of photocopiable page 94 and ask them to identify the 'crooked man', the 'crooked house', the 'crooked stick' and so on. Discuss with the children what is happening in the picture and encourage them to look carefully to see if they can spot the five differences between the two illustrations.

Movements

Objective
To explore the meaning of 'crooked' using physical interpretation.

What you need
A copy of the rhyme 'There was a crooked man', a room with enough space for the children to move freely and safely.

What to do
Say the rhyme 'There was a crooked man' together. Talk with the children about the appearance of the crooked characters. Inspire the children's imagination during movement sessions by asking 'How would the crooked man walk, skip and run?', 'How would the crooked cat, prowl, scamper or jump?' Encourage the children to act out the movements using their whole body to convey the meaning of 'crooked'. Invite

them to suggest actions for the 'crooked mouse'. Develop the theme by asking the children to play Follow-My-Leader or 'mirror' the action of a partner.

Follow-up
• Introduce rhythmic music to motivate dance using 'crooked', 'spiky' and 'jerky' movements. A percussion instrument can be used to stimulate sudden changes in direction, body shape or style of movement.
• Develop the theme by asking the children to dance in pairs with one child playing the 'crooked man' and the other the 'crooked cat'.

A 'crooked mile'

Objective
To involve the children in creating and using a crooked route.

What you need
A copy of the rhyme 'There was a crooked man', a playground, chalk, bicycles, scooters, pedal cars.

What to do
Say the rhyme 'There was a crooked man' together. Talk with the children about the words 'walked a crooked mile' then invite them to create a 'crooked mile' by chalking a long zig-zag line across the playground or other outside area. Encourage them to follow the line by walking, striding, skipping or hopping. Challenge the children to ride their bicycles, pedal cars, scooters and so on along the 'crooked mile'. Encourage them to ride very carefully, keeping as near as they possibly can to the chalk line.

Follow-up
• Let the children help to add obstacles along their crooked route for them to walk 'around', 'over', 'under', 'between', 'along', 'through'.
• Read *Rosie's Walk* by Pat Hutchins (Picture Puffin) to reinforce understanding of the above prepositions.

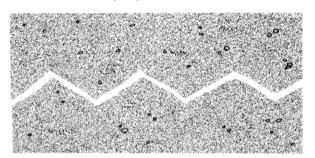

Number game

Objective
To develop number recognition.

What you need
A copy of the rhyme 'There was a crooked man', paper, pens, paints, paintbrushes, scissors, a die or a wooden brick and sticky labels.

What to do
Say the rhyme 'There was a crooked man'. Talk about the words 'little crooked house' and encourage a group of children to paint a large picture of a crooked house. Ask them to paint the 'crooked door', four 'crooked windows' and a 'crooked chimney' on six separate sheets of paper. Let the children help to label each picture with a different number (the numbers will depend on the age and ability of the children) and then involve them in making a die by attaching dots or figures on to a wooden brick. Make sure the values on the die match those written on the door, windows and chimney.

To play
This is a game for two to four children. The first player should throw the die. If, say, a 3 is shown that player must collect picture number 3 and place it on the crooked house. The players take turns to throw the die and place the features of the house. The aim of the game is to complete the picture.

Follow-up
● Reinforce addition or subtraction skills by using two dice.
● Make the game more competitive by organising two teams, each with a 'crooked house' to assemble. The team to complete the house first are the winners.
● Invite the children to draw their own two-dimensional pictures of a crooked house. Encourage them to add 'flaps' which open and close to represent the windows and doors.
● Let the children use craft materials to construct a three-dimensional model of a 'crooked house'.

Crooked characters

Objective
To encourage creative skills and language development.

What you need
A copy of the rhyme 'There was a crooked man', pipe-cleaners, wool, scissors.

What to do
Say the rhyme 'There was a crooked man' together. Discuss the meaning of the word 'crooked'. Let the children use their imagination to create a 'crooked man', a 'crooked cat' and a 'crooked mouse' using pipe-cleaners. Help them to attach

a length of wool to the top of each character so that they can be held in a similar way to a string puppet.
  Next, invite the children to make a simple 'mini theatre' for their 'crooked characters' using a single sheet of folded card, as shown in the illustration. The scenery could depict the 'crooked mile', the 'crooked stile' and the 'crooked house'. Let the children make up their own stories and rhymes as they manoeuvre their 'crooked characters' in front of their 'mini theatre'.

Follow-up
● Help the children to record their stories and rhymes on tape or in writing. Compile their written work in a 'crooked book'.
● Encourage the children to organise short puppet shows for their peers.
● Invite the children to make three-dimensional model puppets using a selection of craft materials.

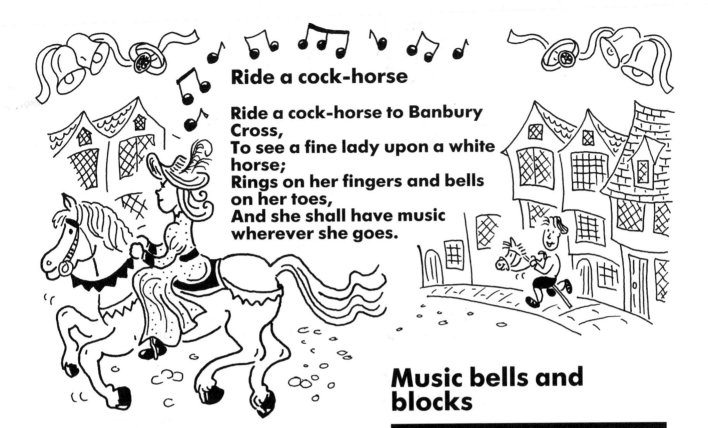

Ride a cock-horse

Ride a cock-horse to Banbury
Cross,
To see a fine lady upon a white
horse;
Rings on her fingers and bells
on her toes,
And she shall have music
wherever she goes.

Join the dots

Objective
To stimulate the children's interest in the rhyme and motivate discussion and observation.

What you need
A copy of the rhyme 'Ride a cock-horse', a copy of photocopiable page 95 for each child, pencils, crayons, felt-tipped pens.

What to do
Say the rhyme 'Ride a cock-horse' together. Provide each child with a copy of photocopiable page 95 and ask them to follow the numbers in the correct order to join the dots. When they have done this, discuss with the children what is happening in the picture.

Music bells and blocks

Objective
To motivate the children to use simple percussion instruments to make music.

What you need
Bells, triangles, woodblocks, rhythm sticks.

What to do
Say the rhyme 'Ride a cock-horse' together and talk about the sounds you might hear as the lady rides along the road, for example the 'clip-clop' of the horse and the jingle of the bells. Let the children hold some bells while they 'ride' around the room; rhythm sticks or woodblocks can be used to create the sound of the horse's hooves.

Invite the children to play their instruments while singing the rhyme, then develop the theme further by asking them to arrange their own piece of music using a combination of bells and woodblocks, triangles and rhythm sticks.

Follow-up

• Make a tape-recording of the children singing rhymes and playing their instruments. Use the tape to complement a nursery rhymes book drawn and written by the children.
• Introduce percussion instruments such as shakers, scrapers, tambourines and hand drums and encourage the children to use them to create original music.
• Invite the children to make their own musical instruments using a wide selection of craft materials.

Making jewellery

Objective

To encourage the children's creative skills.

What you need

A copy of the rhyme 'Ride a cock-horse', card, a hole punch, wool, a selection of beads, small bells, thread, a safety pin or Velcro.

What to do

Say the rhyme 'Ride a cock-horse' together and talk with the children about the 'rings' and 'bells' worn by the 'fine lady upon the white horse'. Invite them to make their own piece of jewellery, for example, a brooch or badge, decorated with beads and bells. To do this, encourage the children to cut a card shape, approximately 5cm square. If you have a hole punch which is safe for children to use, let them punch their own holes in the card shape – three to five holes is sufficient (the position of the holes is unimportant). Next, invite the children to thread a selection of colourful beads and bells on to lengths of wool and then thread these through the holes in the

card. Add Velcro or a safety pin to the back of the card so that the brooch or badge can be worn.

Follow-up

• Invite the children to make their own beads using cut straws, covered buttons or painted and varnished clay.
• Encourage the children to make other items of jewellery by threading their own beads.
• Talk about taking care of special things.
• Invite the children to make a jewellery box or treasure box.
• Let the children wear their jewellery during imaginative play (avoid necklaces and chokers).

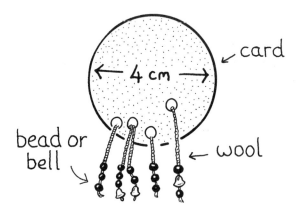

Old-fashioned clothes

Objective

To develop children's awareness of times gone by.

What you need

A copy of the rhyme 'Ride a cock-horse', photographs or pictures of people from the late Victorian era, dressing-up clothes which include long skirts, shawls, top hats, waistcoats and jackets.

What to do

Say the rhyme 'Ride a cock-horse' together. Encourage the children to share ideas about what the 'fine lady' looked like and what she might have worn. Remind them that the rhyme was made up a long time ago, when people wore clothes which were different from those worn today. Show the children some pictures or very old photographs of people in the past. Let the children have fun dressing up in 'old-fashioned' clothes.

Follow-up

● If possible, use a black and white film to take photographs of the children while wearing their dressing-up clothes. When developed use these to stimulate discussion and help the children make a decorative frame for their picture.
● Arrange a special day when the children can come to school or nursery in fancy dress, best clothes or, if it applies, in non-school uniform.
● Invite a grandparent or an old person known to the children to visit the school. Ask them to talk about their memories of the past. School day experiences are particularly fascinating.

Making a hobby horse

Objective

To encourage the children to create a 'toy' which can be used.

What you need

A copy of the rhyme 'Ride a cock-horse', broomsticks, white card, scissors, adhesive, thick felt-tipped pens, decorative threads, ribbons, lace, wool, fur fabric.

What to do

Say the rhyme 'Ride a cock-horse' together and ask the children to imagine how the 'fine lady' may have decorated her white horse for the parade. Invite them to make a decorative hobby horse of their own for use in a classroom parade.

Provide each child with two shapes, cut from white card, which resemble a horse's head and neck. Help them to stick the shapes together, leaving an opening in the base of the neck, through which a broomstick can be placed at a later stage. Encourage the children to draw an eye on both sides of the horse's head using a felt-tipped pen then allow them a high degree of independence as they decorate the horse's head using a colourful array of ribbons and lace. Some children may wish to use the materials to create colourful reins.

Invite the children to 'ride' their 'horses' on a parade around the school grounds. Make this a special occasion by allowing them to wear jewellery they have made, their old-fashioned or fancy clothes and, if possible, provide bells for them to hold.

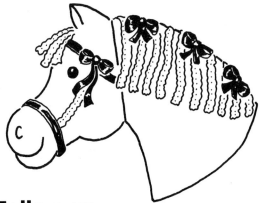

Follow-up

Develop the theme of 'riding' during movement sessions. Encourage the children to imitate riding a horse. Ask them to trot when you call 'green', stop when you call 'red' and jump when you call 'blue'. Add other colours and actions as suggested by the children.

Humpty Dumpty

**Humpty Dumpty sat on a wall,
Humpty Dumpty had a great fall.
All the king's horses and all the king's men,
Couldn't put Humpty together again.**

A Humpty jigsaw

Objective
To stimulate the children's interest in the nursery rhyme and motivate discussion and observation.

What you need
A copy of the rhyme 'Humpty Dumpty', a copy of photocopiable page 96 for each child, coloured pencils, crayons or felt-tipped pens.

What to do
Say the rhyme 'Humpty Dumpty' together. Provide each child with a copy of photocopiable page 96 and ask them to identify the characters shown. Discuss with the children what is happening in the picture and then encourage them to colour it in and cut it into four pieces to use as a jigsaw puzzle.

Sewing a Humpty Dumpty

Objective
To give the children the experience of designing and making a soft toy.

What you need
A selection of non-fraying fabric (each piece cut into a rectangle, approximately 25 x 35cm), sewing thread, needles, soft toy stuffing, small pieces of coloured felt, fabric scissors, paper (approximately 25 x 35cm), pencils, fabric adhesive (such as Copydex).

What to do
Encourage the children to make a Humpty 'pattern' by drawing an egg shape on to paper and cutting it out (approximately 20 x 30cm). Assist the children in pinning their paper pattern on

to two rectangles of non-fraying fabric and in cutting out two fabric 'eggs'. Help them to sew their fabric 'eggs' together, leaving a gap for stuffing. When the children have 'stuffed' their 'egg' help them to sew up the gap. Let them cut out shapes from felt to represent eyes, mouth, buttons, arms, legs and so on (see Figure 1).

Each 'Humpty Dumpty' will develop its own character and style as the children secure their felt 'features' in place using fabric adhesive.

Follow-up
● Use the soft toys to encourage imaginative play.
● Let the children construct a 'wall' from a small box for their soft toy to 'sit on'.

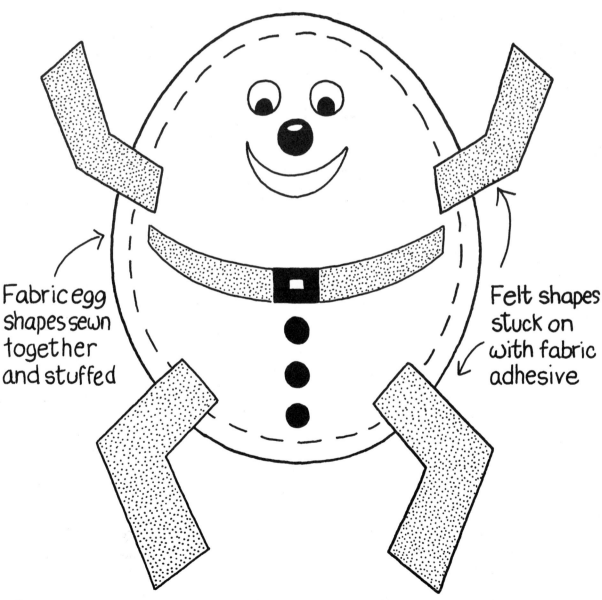

Fabric egg shapes sewn together and stuffed

Felt shapes stuck on with fabric adhesive

Figure 1

Constructing brick walls

Objective
To increase children's awareness about how a brick wall is built.

What you need
A copy of the rhyme 'Humpty Dumpty', wooden or plastic building blocks, a real brick wall within close distance of the classroom, paper, crayons, pencils.

What to do
Say the rhyme 'Humpty Dumpty' together. Talk about the words 'sat on a wall' and ask the children to imagine Humpty's wall. Is it high or low? Is it long or short? Is it in a garden, a castle or town? Take the children on a walk to look at real brick walls nearby. Encourage them to observe the patterns created when bricks are laid together. Invite the children to take rubbings and draw pictures of the walls. Back indoors invite the children to experiment building walls of their own using large blocks based on their drawings.

Follow-up
• Encourage the children to build a wall low enough to step over, high enough to hide behind and wide enough to lay on.
• Play a game similar to skittles using 'mini brick' walls and a soft sponge ball to knock them down.
• Read the story of 'The Three Little Pigs'.

Falling over

Objective
To encourage discussion and consideration of others.

What you need
A copy of the rhyme 'Humpty Dumpty', a comfortable place to sit.

What to do
Say the rhyme 'Humpty Dumpty' together. Talk about the words 'had a great fall' and ask the children what this means. Invite them to talk about their own experiences of falling over or falling from a height. Let the children share ideas about how they would help someone who has fallen over.

Follow-up
• Visit the school medical room with the children and talk to the person who tends to cuts and grazes.
• Turn the home corner into a 'doctor's surgery' or 'medical room' to motivate imaginative play.

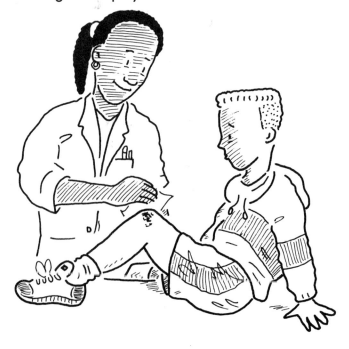

Our caring hands

Compiling a first aid kit

Objective
To develop the children's awareness of the need to help others.

What you need
A copy of the rhyme 'Humpty Dumpty', plasters, antiseptic cream, cotton wool, small bandages, tissue, scissors, a plastic tub with lid, red sticky tape or a label and red pen.

What to do
Begin by saying the rhyme 'Humpty Dumpty' together and talk with the children about what they could do to make Humpty feel better after falling off the wall. Relate this to their own experiences of having cuts and grazes tended to.

Invite the children to compile a first aid kit for helping children who have hurt themselves. Let them place the plasters, creams and so on into a container and invite them to stick or draw a red cross on the lid. Talk about the different uses of each item in the first aid kit and for what reasons they could be used.

Follow-up
● Invite the school nurse in to talk to the children.
● Encourage the children to talk about how they can help each other if one of them falls over in the playground or while out playing at home.
● Invite the children to talk about 'caring hands'. What can our hands do to help others?
● Encourage the children to draw around their hand on to coloured paper and then write or draw a picture on the hand shape about someone they care for. Display all the hands together to form a 'caring hands circle', 'caring hands heart' or 'caring hands tree'.

Feelings, see page 14

What are they feeling and why?

How animals change and grow, see page 32

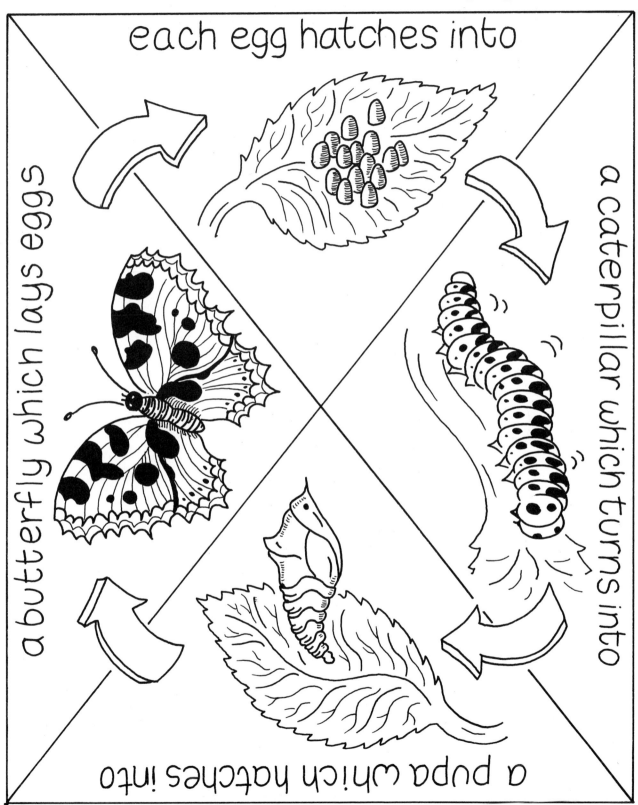

each egg hatches into

a caterpillar which turns into

a pupa which hatches into

a butterfly which lays eggs

The chicken and the egg, see page 33

a chicken,

lays an egg

the chick grows inside the egg

the chick hatches,

and the chick grows up into

a chicken

Do pets have toys? see page 52

	1	2	3	4	5	6	7	8
Cat								
Dog								
Hamster								
Mouse								
Rabbit								
Tortoise								
Gerbil								

A sorting and naming game, see page 58

Red Yellow Green Blue

Wheeled vehicle survey, see page 68

	car
	bus
	milkfloat
	motorbike
	bicycle
	ambulance
	fire engine
	lorry
	ice-cream van
	van

Spot the difference, see page 78

Join the dots, see page 81

A Humpty jigsaw, see page 84